Lotus

Illustrated DICTIONARY of LITERATURE

Complied and Edited by:
Jack Richardson

Lotus PRESS
4735/22, Prakash Deep Building
Ansari Road, Darya Ganj,
New Delhi-110002

Lotus Illustrated

DICTIONARY of LITERATURE

ISBN 81 89093 43 6

Published by:

Lotus Press : Publishers & Distributors

Unit No. 220, 2nd Floor, 4735/22,

Prakash Deep Building, Ansari Road, Darya Ganj,

New Delhi- 110002, Ph.: 32903912, 23280047, 09811838000

• E-mail : lotus_press@sify.com www.lotuspress.co.in

Printed at : A.J. Book Binding House, Delhi

Preface

More than two thousand years ago, the Roman poet Horace claimed that literature is 'sweet' and 'useful'. Since then, literature has been traditionally understood, at least in Western cultures, as having the dual purpose of entertaining and educating its audience. Literary texts are constructed in effect as objects of beauty, sources of pleasure and as conveyors of messages and information. While authors often claim no practical purpose for their works, all literature constitutes an attempt at persuasively conveying certain values and ideas. The entertaining and beautiful aspect of literary works acts in reality as part of the appeal and attractiveness, which the work tries to attach to the ideas, which it seeks to convey. The beauty of literature is therefore a part of its rhetoric, a device intended to strengthen the overall persuasiveness and influence of the work on its audience. While the entertaining aspect of literature may be rather obvious, understanding the ideas or values which a text advances is not always a simple task. Part of the problem is the fact that the ideas of a literary text are almost always presented in indirect or 'symbolic' form.

We all are aware about the fact that writing about literature is not be easy if we haven't learned to read literature, for in order to write about anything you have to know that something rather well. Helping you learn to read literature is what we hope to achieve through this dictionary. This dictionary is a storehouse of all the literary terms.

abecedarian poem

a poem having verses beginning with the successive letters of the alphabet.

abstract

used as a noun, the term refers to a short summary or outline of a longer work. As an adjective applied to writing or literary works. Abstract refers to words or phrases that name things not knowable through the five senses. Examples of abstracts include the 'Cliffs Notes' summaries of major literary works. Examples of abstract terms or concepts include 'idea', 'guilt' 'honesty' and 'loyalty'.

abstract language

words that represent ideas, intangibles and concepts such as 'beauty' and 'truth'.

abstract poetry

poetry that aims to use its sounds, textures, rhythms and rhymes to convey an emotion, instead of relying on the meanings of words.

absurd theatre

see **theatre of the absurd.**

absurdism

see **theatre of the absurd.**

academic verse

poetry that adheres to the accepted standards and requirements of some kind of 'school'. Poetry approved, officially, or unofficially, by a literary establishment.

acatalectic

a verse having a metrically complete number of syllables in the final foot.

accent

1. the emphasis or stress placed on a syllable in poetry. Traditional poetry commonly uses patterns of accented and unaccented syllables (known as feet) that create distinct rhythms. Much modern poetry uses less formal arrangements that create a sense of freedom and spontaneity. The following line from William Shakespeare's 'Hamlet':

'to be or not to be: that is the question'

has five accents, on the words 'be', 'not', 'be' and 'that', and the first syllable of 'question'.

2. the rhythmically significant stress in the articulation of words, giving some syllables more relative prominence than others. In words of two or more syllables, one syllable is almost invariably stressed more strongly than the other syllables. In words of one syllable, the degree of stress normally depends on their grammatical function; nouns, verbs and adjectives are usually given more stress than articles or prepositions. The words in a line of poetry are usually arranged so the accents occur at regular intervals, with the meter defined by the placement of the accents within the foot. Accent should not be construed as emphasis.

3. the emphasis, or stress, given to a syllable in pronunciation.

Accents can also be used to emphasise a particular word in a sentence.

■ **accentual meter**

a rhythmic pattern based on a recurring number of accents or stresses in each line of a poem or section of a poem.

■ **accentual verse**

lines whose rhythm arises from its stressed syllables rather than from the number of its syllables, or from the length of time devoted to their sounding. Old English poems such as Beowulf and Caedmon's Hymn are accentual. They fall clearly into two halves, each with two stresses.

■ **accentual-syllabic verse**

the normal system of verse composition in England since the fourteenth century, in which the meter depends upon counting both the number of stresses and the total number of syllables in any given line. An iambic pentameter for example contains five stressed syllables and a total of ten syllables.

■ **acephalexis**

initial truncation (the dropping of the first, unstressed syllable at the beginning of a line of iambic or anapaestic verse).

■ **acephalous (Greek 'headless')**

a line of verse without its expected initial syllable.

■ **acrostic**

1. a poem in which the first letter of each line spells out a name (downwards).

2. a word, phrase, or passage spelled out vertically by the first letters of a group of lines in sequence. Sir John Davies' 'Hymns of Astraea' dedicates 26 acrostic poems to Elizabeth I.

■ **act**

a major section of a play. Acts are divided into varying numbers of shorter scenes. From the ancient times to the nineteenth century, plays were generally constructed of five acts, but modern works typically consist of one, two, or three acts. Examples of five-act plays include the works of Sophocles and Shakespeare, while the plays of Arthur Miller commonly have a three-act structure. The ends of acts are typically indicated by lowering the curtain or turning up the houselights. Playwrights frequently employ acts to accommodate changes in time, setting, characters onstage, or mood. In many full-length plays, acts are further divided into scenes, which often mark a point in the action when the location changes or when a new character enters.

■ **acto**

a one-act Chicano theatre piece developed out of collective improvisation.

adonic

a verse consisting of a dactyl followed by a spondee or trochee.

adynaton

a type of hyperbole in which the exaggeration is magnified so greatly that it refers to an impossibility, for example, 'I'd walk a million miles for one of your smiles'.

aesthetic movement

a literary belief that art is its own justification and purpose, advocated in England by Walter Pater and practiced by Edgar Allan Poe, Algernon Charles Swinburne and others.

aestheticism

a literary and artistic movement of the nineteenth century. Followers of the movement believed that art should not be mixed with social, political, or moral teaching. The statement 'art for art's sake' is a good summary of aestheticism. The movement had its roots in France, but it gained widespread importance in England in the last half of the nineteenth century, where it helped change the Victorian practice of including moral lessons in literature.

Oscar Wilde is one of the best-known 'aesthetes' of the late nineteenth century.

affective fallacy

an error in judging the merits or faults of a work of literature. The 'error' results from stressing the importance of the work's effect upon the reader — that is, how it makes a reader 'feel' emotionally, what it does as a literary work — instead of stressing its inner qualities as a created object, or what it 'is'.

The affective fallacy is evident in Aristotle's precept from his 'Poetics' that the purpose of tragedy is to evoke 'fear and pity' in its spectators. Also known as sympathetic fallacy.

afflatus

a creative inspiration, as that of a poet; a divine imparting of knowledge, thus it is often called divine afflatus.

Age of Johnson

the period in English literature between 1750 and 1798, named after the most prominent literary figure of the age, Samuel Johnson. Works written during this time are noted for their emphasis on 'sensibility' or emotional quality. These works formed a transition between the rational works of the Age of Reason, or Neoclassical period and the emphasis on individual feelings and responses of the Romantic period.

Significant writers during the Age of Johnson included the novelists Ann Radcliffe and Henry Mackenzie, dramatists Richard Sheridan and Oliver Goldsmith and poets William Collins and Thomas Gray.

Also known as Age of Sensibility.

Henry Mackenzie

■ Age of Sensibility

see **Age of Johnson.**

■ agrarians

a group of Southern American writers of the 1930s and 1940s who fostered an economic and cultural program for the South, based on agriculture, in opposition to the industrial society of the North. The term can refer to any group that promotes the value of farm life and agricultural society.

Members of the original Agrarians included John Crowe Ransom, Allen Tate and Robert Penn Warren.

Robert Penn Warren

■ alazon

a deceiving or self-deceived character in fiction, normally an object of ridicule in comedy or satire, but often the hero of a tragedy. In comedy, he most frequently takes the form of a pedant.

■ Albert Camus (1913–60)

Albert Camus was a French writer, a famous author and thinker of the 20th century. When he was a student at the University of Algiers, he formed a theatre group and adapted, directed and acted in plays. He actively participated in social reforms and was a member of the Communist party for a brief period of time. Shortly after his essay Noces appeared (1939), he went to Paris as a journalist. He was also the part of the French struggle in World War II and was. The principal editor of the underground paper Combat.

His writings were famous for his vigorous, concise and lucid style. His essay Le Mythe de Sisyphe formulates his theory of the absurd and is the philosophical basis of his novel *L'Étranger* and of his plays *Le Malentendu* and *Caligula*. He was awarded the Nobel Prize for Literature in 1957. He died in a car crash in 1960.

■ alcaic verse

a Greek lyrical meter, said to be invented by Alcaeus, a lyric poet from about 600 B.C. Written in tetrameter, the greater Alcaic consists of a spondee or iamb, followed by an iamb plus a long syllable and two dactyls. The lesser Alcaic, also in tetrameter, consists of two dactylic feet, followed by two iambic feet.

■ alcaics

a four-line Classical stanza named after Alcaeus, a Greek poet, with a predominantly dactylic meter, imitated by Alfred lord Tennyson's poem, Milton.

Alfred Lord Tennyson

■ Aleksandr Sergeyevich Pushkin (1799-1837)

Aleksandr Sergeyevich Pushkin, was a Russian poet and prose writer. He was among the foremost figures in Russian literature. He was exiled in 1820 because of ideas expressed in his *Ode to Liberty* and his satirical verse portraits of figures at court. In 1820, his fairy romance *Russlan and Ludmilla* was published. He was strongly moved by the beauty of the Crimea and the Caucasus and wrote two poems describing its beauty, *The Prisoner of the Caucasus* (1822) and *The Fountain of Bakhchisarai* (1824). Pushkin's yearning for freedom is expressed through *The Gypsies* (1823–24). He used Russian history as the basis of his work. Some of his poems on this theme are *Poltava* (1828) and *The Bronze Horseman* (1833). He also wrote two short novels on this theme, *The Captain's Daughter* (1837) and *The History of the Pugachev Rebellion* (1834). *Eugene Onegin* (1823–31), a novel in verse concerning mutually rejected love is considered as his masterpiece. Pushkin's other major works include the dramas *Mozart and Salieri* and *The Stone Guest* (both 1830), the folktale *The Golden Cockerel* (1833) and the short stories *Tales by Belkin* (1831) and *The Queen of Spades* (1834).

■ Alexander Pope (1688-1744)

Alexander Pope was the greatest English poet as well as verse satirist of the 18th century. Pope's poetry falls into three periods. The first includes the early descriptive poetry like the *Pastorals* (1709), *Windsor Forest* (1713), *the Essay on Criticism* (1711), *The Rape of the Lock* (1714). This phase also includes his only two pieces dealing with love, *Elegy to the Memory of an Unfortunate Lady* and *Eloise to Abelard.* Pope's second period includes his magnificent, if somewhat inaccurate, translations of Homer. The completed version of *The Iliad* came out in 1720 and *The Odyssey* was published somewhere between 1725-26. In the last period of his career, Pope turned to writing satires and moral poems, which include *The Dunciad* (1728–43), *Imitations of Horace* (1733–38), his most ambitious work, *Moral Essays* (1731–35) and the *Epistle to Arbuthnot* (1735), a defense in poetry of his life and his work.

Alexandre Dumas (1802–70)

he is more commonly known as Dumas père. Alexandre Dumas was a famous French novelist and dramatist. His father was a general in the Revolution. Many generations of readers were delighted with his highly romantic novels canonising *The adventures of the Three Musketeers* and *The Count of Monte Cristo*. Duma was an ostentatious youth, marked with a gift for storytelling and an affinity towards love affairs. At the age of 20, he obtained a minor post with the duc d'Orléans in Paris and later became active in the Revolution of 1830.

His initial achievements were the historical dramas *Henri III et sa cour* (1829), *Christine* (1830), *Antony* (1831) and *La Tour de Nesle* (1832). *Queen Margot* (1845), *The Lady of Monsoreau* (1846), *The Forty-Five* (1848), *The Black Tulip* (1850) and *The Journal of Madame Giovanni* (1944) are some of his other works. He was interested in Italian unification and took an active part in Garibaldi's expedition in 1860.

Alexandrine

1. an iambic line of twelve syllables, or six feet, usually with a caesura after the sixth syllable. It is the standard line in French poetry, comparable to the iambic pentameter line in English poetry.

2. a metrical line of six feet or twelve syllables (in English), originally from French heroic verse. Randle Cotgrave, in his 1611 French-English dictionary, explains: 'Alexandrin. A verse of 12, or 13 syllables'. In his Essay on Criticism, Alexander Pope says, 'A needless Alexandrine ends the song

Alexander Pope

/ That like a wounded snake, drags its slow length along' (359). Examples include Michael Drayton's Polyolbion, Robert Bridges' Testament of Beauty and the last line of each stanza in Thomas Hardy's The Convergence of the Twain.

Robert Bridges

■ allegory

1. a narrative technique in which characters representing things or abstract ideas are used to convey a message or teach a lesson. Allegory is typically used to teach moral, ethical, or religious lessons but is sometimes used for satiric or political purposes.

Examples of allegorical works include Edmund Spenser's 'The Faerie Queene' and John Bunyan's 'The Pilgrim's Progress'.

2. a figurative illustration of truths or generalisations about human conduct or experience in a narrative or description, by the use of symbolic fictional figures and actions which resemble the subject's properties and circumstances.

John Bunyan

■ alliteration

a poetic device where the first consonant sounds or any vowel sounds in words or syllables are repeated.

The following description of the Green Knight from the anonymous 'Sir Gawain and the Green Knight' gives an example of alliteration:

And in *g*uise all of *g*reen, the *g*ear and the man:

A *c*oat *c*ut *c*lose, that *c*lung to his sides

An a *m*antle to *m*atch, *m*ade with a lining

Of *f*urs cut and *f*itted — the *f*abric was noble....

■ allusion

a reference to a familiar literary or historical person or event, used to make an idea more easily understood.

For example, describing someone as a 'Romeo' makes an allusion to William Shakespeare's famous young lover in 'Romeo and Juliet'.

■ Ama Ata Aidoo (1942)

Ama Ata Aidoo was a Ghanaian author, poet and playwright. She was educated in the University of Ghana (B.A., 1964). She writes about the contemporary roles of African women and the negative impact of Western influences on African culture, by combining traditional African storytelling with Western genres. In 1965, her first play *The Dilemma of a Ghost* was published. Her collection of short stories *No Sweetness Here* (1970) and *The Girl Who Can* (1997) and her novel, *Our Sister Killjoy* (1977), expand on these themes. Many of her works reflect her own experiences. Her other works include the play *Anowa* (1980), the poems of *Someone Talking to Sometime* (1985), *Birds* (1987) and *Angry Letter in January* (1992), *a collection of children's stories* (1986) and the novel Changes: *A Love Story* (1991), tells about the contemporary African marriage.

■ ambiguity

allows for two or more simultaneous interpretations of a word, phrase, action or situation, all of which can be supported by the context of a work. Deliberate ambiguity can contribute to the effectiveness and richness of a work, for example, in the open-ended conclusion to Hawthorne's Young Goodman Brown. However, unintentional ambiguity obscures meaning and can confuse readers.

■ Amerind literature

the writing and oral traditions of Native Americans. Native American literature was originally passed on by word of mouth, so it consisted largely of stories and events that were easily memorised. Amerind prose is often rhythmic like poetry because it was recited to the beat of a ceremonial drum.

Examples of Amerind literature include the autobiographical 'Black Elk Speaks', the works of N. Scott Momaday, James Welch and Craig Lee Strete and the poetry of Luci Tapahonso.

Luxi Tapahonso

■ Amiri Baraka (1934)

Amiri Baraka is an American poet, playwright and political activist. In 1964, four of his plays—*Dutch-*

man, The Toilet, The Baptism and *The Slave*—were produced Off-Broadway in New York City, for which he gained notoriety. A provocative political analyst, he has written many works that express a strident anger towards the racism of mainstream white American society. His volumes of poems include *Preface to a Twenty Volume Suicide Note* (1961), *Selected Poetry* (1979), *Transbluesency: The Selected Poems of Amiri Baraka/LeRoi Jones, 1961–1995* (1995) and *Eulogies* (1996), among his many plays are *The Motion of History and Other Plays* (1978) and *Election-Machine Warehouse* (1996), his volumes of essays include *Blues People: Negro Music in White America* (1963) and *Daggers and Javelins* (1984). He edited *Confirmation: An Anthology of African-American Women* (1983) with his second wife Amina Baraka. In 1965, Baraka founded Harlem's Black Arts Repertory Theatre. He has taught at a number of colleges and universities. His collection of fiction was published in 2000.

■ amphibrach

a metrical foot consisting of a long or accented syllable between two short or unaccented syllables.

■ amphigouri

a verse composition, which is although apparently coherent, contains no sense or meaning.

■ amplification

the use of bare expressions, likely to be ignored or misunderstood by a hearer or reader because of the bluntness. Emphasis through restatement with additional details.

■ anachronism

the placement of an event, person, or thing out of its proper chronological relationship, sometimes unintentional, but often deliberate as an exercise of poetic license.

■ anaclasis

the substitution of different measures to break up the rhythm.

■ anacreontic

a poem in the style of the Greek poet, Anacreon, convivial in tone or theme, relating to the praise of love and wine.

■ anacrusis

when one or more unstressed syllables are added at the beginning of a line.

■ anagogic

relating to literature as a total order of words.

■ anagram

a word or phrase made from the letters of another word or phrase, as 'heart' is an anagram of 'earth'. Anagrams have often been considered merely an exercise of one's ingenuity, but sometimes writers use anagrams to conceal proper names or veiled messages, or to suggest important connections between words, as in 'hated' and 'death'.

■ **analogy**

a comparison of two things, made to explain something unfamiliar through its similarities to something familiar, or to prove one point based on the acceptance of another. Similes and metaphors are types of analogies.

Analogies often take the form of an extended simile, as in William Blake's aphorism: 'As the caterpillar chooses the fairest leaves to lay her eggs on, so the priest lays his curse on the fairest joys'.

William Blake

■ **anapest**

a metrical foot consisting of three syllables. The first two are unstressed and the last is stressed: 'di di dum'.

■ **anaphora**

the repetition of an opening word or phrase in a number of lines.

■ **anastrophe**

a type of hyperbaton involving the inversion of the natural or usual syntactical order of a pair of words for a rhetorical or poetic effect.

■ **anatomy**

a form of prose fiction, traditionally known as the Menippean or Varronian satire and represented by Burton's Anatomy of Melancholy, characterised by a great variety of subject-matter and a strong interest in ideas. In shorter forms, it often has a cena or symposium setting and verse interludes.

■ **angry young men**

a group of British writers of the 1950s whose work expressed bitterness and disillusionment with society. Common to their work is an anti-hero who rebels against a corrupt social order and strives for personal integrity.

The term has been used to describe Kingsley Amis, John Osborne, Colin Wilson, John Wain and others.

Kingsley Anis

■ **Anita Brookner (1928-)**

Anita Brookner was a well-known English writer and art

critic. She was the first woman appointed (1968) as a Slade Professor of Art at Cambridge. After establishing an academic career at London's Courtauld Institute of Art, she began writing fiction in 1980, producing approximately one book a year. Her quiet, often bleak novels usually concern meek and genteel middle-aged women, unfortunate in love and largely unable to establish relationships with those around them. Her major works are *Look at Me* (1983), *Hotel du Lac* (1984, Booker Prize), *Latecomers* (1988), *Fraud* (1992), *Undue Influence* (1999) and *The Bay of Angels* (2001). Her non-fiction work *Romanticism and Its Discontents* (2000) is an analysis of French Romanticism.

■ antagonist

the major character in a narrative or drama, who works against the hero or protagonist.

An example of an evil antagonist is Richard Lovelace in Samuel Richardson's 'Clarissa', while a virtuous antagonist is Macduff in William Shakesp-eare's 'Macbeth'.

■ antanaclasis

a figure of speech in which the same word is repeated in a different sense within a clause or line.

■ anthology

a collection of selected literary, artistic, or musical works or parts of works.

■ Anthony Burgess (1917–93)

He was an English novelist, born in Manchester as John Anthony Burgess Wilson. He graduated from Manchester University in 1940. He worked as a teacher in England and in East Asia and pursued an early interest in music. His novels are marked by an unreal, mysteriously comic imagination. He is recognised to have been one of the most imaginative and experimental English prose stylists. Burgess's best-known work is *A Clockwork Orange* (1962) that is written in an imaginary teen slang and set in a classless futuristic society, where an intelligent young hoodlum asserts his individuality by deliberately choosing to do evil. His other works include the novels *Inside Mr. Enderby* (1961), *MF* (1971), *Napoleon Symphony: A Novel in Four Movements* (1974), *Earthly Powers* (1980), *The Devil's Mode* (1989) and the posthumously published *A Dead Man in Deptford* (1995) and *Byrne* (1997), as well as a study of James Joyce, *Re Joyce* (1968).

■ anthropomorphism

the presentation of animals or objects in human shape or with human characteristics. The term is derived from the Greek word for 'human form'.

'The Fables of Aesop', the animated films of Walt Disney and Richard Adams's 'Watership Down' feature anthropomorphic characters.

■ **antibacchius**

a metrical foot consisting of two long syllables followed by a short syllable.

■ **anticlimax**

the intentional use of elevated language to describe the trivial or commonplace, or a sudden transition from a significant thought to a trivial one, in order to achieve a humorous or satiric effect.

■ **anti-hero**

a protagonist who has the opposite of most of the traditional attributes of a hero. He or she may be bewildered, ineffectual, deluded, or merely pathetic. Often what antiheroes learn, if they learn anything at all, is that the world isolates them in an existence devoid of God and absolute values. Yossarian from Joseph Heller's 'Catch-22' is an example of an antihero.

Joseph Heller

■ **antimasque**

see **masque.**

■ **anti-novel**

a term coined by French critic Jean-Paul Sartre. It refers to any experimental work of fiction that avoids the familiar conventions of the novel. The anti-novel usually fragments and distorts the experience of its characters, forcing the reader to construct the reality of the story from a disordered narrative.

The best-known anti-novelist is Alain Robbe-Grillet, author of 'Le voyeur'.

■ **antiphrasis**

the ironic or humorous use of words in a sense not in accord with their literal meaning, as in 'a giant of three feet four inches'.

■ **antispast**

a metrical foot consisting of two long syllables between two short syllables.

■ **antistrophe**

the second division in the triadic structure of Pindaric verse, corresponding metrically to the strophe; also, the stanza following or alternating with and responding to the strophe in ancient lyric poetry.

■ **antithesis**

the antithesis of something is its direct opposite. In literature, the use of antithesis as a figure of speech results in two statements that show a contrast through the balancing of two opposite ideas. Technically, it is the second portion of the statement that is defined as the 'antithesis'; the first portion is the 'thesis'.

An example of antithesis is found in the following portion of Abraham Lincoln's 'Gettysburg Address'; notice the opposition between the verbs 'remember' and 'forget' and the phrases 'what we say' and 'what they did': 'The world will little note nor long remember what we say here, but it can never forget what they did here'.

■ antonomasia

the use of a name, epithet or title in place of a proper name, as 'Bard' for Shakespeare.

■ antonym

one of two or more words that have opposite meanings.

■ aphaeresis or apheresis

a type of elision in which a letter or syllable is omitted at the beginning of a word, for example *'twas* for *it was*.

■ aphesis

a form of aphaeresis in which the syllable omitted is short and unaccented, as in 'round' for 'around'.

■ aphorism

a brief statement containing an important truth or fundamental principle.

■ apocalyptic

the thematic term corresponding to 'myth' in fictional literature.

■ apocope

a type of elision in which a letter or syllable is omitted at the end of a word, as in 'morn' for 'morning'.

■ apocrypha

writings tentatively attributed to an author but not proven or universally accepted to be their works. The term was originally applied to certain books of the Bible that were not considered inspired and so were not included in the 'sacred canon'.

Geoffrey Chaucer, William Shakespeare, Thomas Kyd, Thomas Middleton and John Marston all have apocrypha. Apocryphal books of the Bible include the Old Testament's Book of Enoch and New Testament's Gospel of Thomas.

■ Apollonian and Dionysian

the two impulses believed to guide authors of dramatic tragedy. The Apollonian impulse is named after Apollo, the Greek god of light and beauty and the symbol of intellectual order. The Dionysian impulse is named after Dionysus, the Greek god of wine and the symbol of the unrestrained forces of nature. The Apollonian impulse is to create a rational, harmonious world, while the Dionysian is to express the irrational forces of personality.

Friedrich Nietzche uses these terms in 'The Birth of Tragedy' to designate contrasting elements in Greek tragedy.

apologue

an allegorical narrative, usually intended to convey a moral or a useful truth.

aposiopesis

stopping short of a complete thought for effect, thus calling attention to it, usually by a sudden breaking off, as in 'He acted like—but I pretended not to notice', leaving the unsaid portion to the reader's imagination.

apostrophe

a statement, question or request addressed to an inanimate object or concept or to a nonexistent or absent person.

Requests for inspiration from the muses in poetry are examples of apostrophe, as is Marc Antony's address to Caesar's corpse in William Shakespeare's 'Julius Caesar': 'O, pardon me, thou bleeding piece of earth, That I am meek and gentle with these butchers!...

Woe to the hand that shed this costly blood!...'

Julius Caesar

apprenticeship novel

see **bildungsroman.**

approximate rhyme

see **rhyme.**

arcadia

a region or scene characterised by idyllic quiet and simplicity, often chosen as a setting for pastoral poetry.

archaism

a word or expression no longer in general use, for example, 'thou mayst' is an archaism meaning, 'you may'.

archetype

the word archetype is commonly used to describe an original pattern or model from which all other things of the same kind are made. This term was introduced to literary criticism from the psychology of Carl Jung. It expresses Jung's theory that behind every person's 'unconscious', or repressed memories of the past, lies the 'collective unconscious' of the human race: memories of the countless typical experiences of our ancestors. These memories are said to prompt illogical associations that trigger powerful emotions in the reader. Often, the emotional process is primitive, even primordial. Archetypes are the literary images that grow out of the 'collective unconscious'. They appear in literature as incidents and plots that repeat basic patterns of life.

They may also appear as stereotyped characters.

Examples of literary archetypes include themes such as birth and death and characters such as the Earth Mother.

argument

the argument of a work is the author's subject matter or principal idea.

Examples of defined 'argument' portions of works include John Milton's 'Arguments' to each of the books of 'Paradise Lost' and the 'Argument' to Robert Herrick's 'Hesperides'.

John Milton

aristotelian criticism

specifically, the method of evaluating and analysing tragedy formulated by the Greek philosopher Aristotle in his 'Poetics'. More generally, the term indicates any form of criticism that follows Aristotle's views. Aristotelian criticism focuses on the form and logical structure of a work, apart from its historical or social context, in contrast to 'Platonic Criticism', which stresses the usefulness of art.

Arnold Bennett (Enoch Arnold Bennett) (1867–1931)

Arnold Bennett is a renowned English novelist and dramatist. He is famous for his realistic novels about the Five Towns, an imaginary manufacturing district in northern England. Bennett's early career included editing the fashionable magazine Woman and writing literary reviews and articles. About 1900, he began to devote himself industriously to his own work, producing a series of excellent regional novels. Influenced by the naturalism of Zola, he depicted in great detail the grim, sometimes sordid, lives of shopkeepers and potters. His attitude towards his characters was one of affectionate sympathy and he always managed to make their mundane lives interesting. Bennett's best work is contained in his novels of the *Five Towns*, which include *Anna of the Five Towns (*1902), *The Old Wives' Tale* (1908), *The Trilogy Clayhanger* (1910), *Hilda Lessways* (1911) and *These Twain* (1916). Bennett also achieved considerable success as a playwright, most notably with *Milestones* (1912), written with Edward Knoblock and *The Great Adventure* (1913).

■ arsis

the accented or longer part of a poetic foot; the point where an ictus is put.

■ art for art's sake

see **aestheticism.**

■ Arthur Miller (1915–)

Arthur Miller was an American dramatist who was born in New York City. He graduated from the University of Michigan in 1938. Miller's plays are concerned with morality and the pressures exerted on people by family and society. His masterpiece, *Death of a Salesman* (1949, Pulitzer Prize), is the story of a salesman betrayed by his own hollow values and those of American society. *The Crucible* (1953) is both a dynamic dramatisation of the 17th-century Salem witch trials and a parable about the United States in the McCarthy era. Miller's life with his second wife, Marilyn Monroe, is fictionalised in his *After the Fall* (1964).

Miller's other plays include *The Man Who Had All the Luck* (1940), *All My Sons* (1947), *Incident at Vichy* (1965), *The Price* (1968), *The Creation of the World and Other Business* (1972), *The Ride down Mount Morgan* (1991) and *Broken Glass* (1994). He has also written a screenplay, *The Misfits* (1961), television dramas, *Playing for Time* (1980) and *Clara* (1991), a novel, *Focus* (1945) and a study of the Soviet Union, *In Russia* (1969), with photographs by his third wife, Inge Morath.

■ Arundhati Roy (1961-)

She is the first Indian citizen to win the prestigious Booker Prize for her world-famous book *The God of Small Things.* This book made Arundhati Roy a celebrity and a tall literary persona. She grew up in Kerala, where her award-winning novel is set. The main theme of the novel is the poetic tale of Indian boy-and-girl twins, Estha and Rahel and their family's tragedies. The story's fulcrum is the death of their 9-year-old half British cousin, Sophie Mol, visiting them on holiday. The novel is a social comedy, three-generation saga and tragic love story—is, most of all, an intensely human drama. It is the tale of how the drowning of a little girl and the police murder of an illicit lover utterly destroys a well-to-do Indian family, especially two children, whose lives are emotionally blasted and withered.

She, with her very youthful appearance, is indeed one of People Magazine's '50 Most Beautiful People in the World 1998'. She won the Booker Prize, Britain's most prestigious literary award, in 1997, for her debut novel, *The God of Small Things.* The novel became a bestseller in more than 25 countries, from India to Germany, from Portugal to the United States. She is now in her late-30s and is currently living in Delhi.

■ aside

a comment made by a stage performer that is intended to be heard by the audience but supposedly not by other characters.

Eugene O'Neill's 'Strange Interlude' is an extended use of the aside in modern theatre.

■ assonance

the repetition of similar vowel sounds in poetry.

The following lines from Gerald Manley Hopkins's 'God's Grandeur' contain several patterns of assonance:

The world is charged with the grandeur of God.

It will flame out, like shining from shook foil;

It gathers to a greatness, like the ooze of oil

Crushed. Why do men then now not reck his rod?

■ asyndeton

the omission of conjunctions that ordinarily join coordinate words and phrases, as in 'see no evil, hear no evil, speak no evil'.

■ aubade

a song or poem with a motif of greeting the dawn, often involving the parting of lovers, or a call for a beloved to arise.

■ audience

the people for whom a piece of literature is written. Authors usually write with a certain audience in mind, for example, children, members of a religious or ethnic group, or colleagues in a professional field. The term 'audience' also applies to the people who gather to see or hear any performance, including plays, poetry readings, speeches and concerts.

■ auto

a form of drama in which the main subject is sacred or sacrosanct legend, such as miracle plays, solemn and processional in form but not strictly tragic.

■ autobiography

a connected narrative in which an individual tells his or her life story.

Examples include Benjamin Franklin's 'Autobiography' and Henry Adams's 'The Education of Henry Adams'.

■ automatic writing

writing carried out without a preconceived plan, in an effort to capture every random thought. Authors who engage in automatic writing typically do not revise their work, preferring instead to preserve the revealed truth and beauty of spontaneous expression.

Automatic writing was employed by many of the Surrealist writers, notably the French poet Robert Desnos.

Robert Desnos

avant-garde

a French term meaning 'vanguard'. It is used in literary criticism to describe new writing that rejects traditional approaches to literature in favour of innovations in style or content.

Twentieth-century examples of the literary 'avant-garde' include 'the Black Mountain School of poets', 'the Bloomsbury Group' and 'the Beat Movement'.

bacchius

in ancient poetry, a metrical foot consisting of a short syllable followed by two long syllables.

ballad

a short poem that tells a simple story and has a repeated refrain. Ballads were originally intended to be sung. Early ballads, known as folk ballads, were passed down through generations, so their authors are often unknown. Later ballads composed by known authors are called literary ballads.

An example of an anonymous folk ballad is 'Edward', which dates from the Middle Ages. Samuel Taylor Coleridge's 'The Rime of the Ancient Mariner' and John Keats's 'La Belle Dame sans Merci' are examples of literary ballads.

Samuel Taylor Coleridge

ballade

frequently represented in French poetry, a fixed form consisting of three, seven or eight-line stanzas using no more than three recurrent rhymes with an identical refrain after each stanza and a closing envoi repeating the rhymes of the last four lines of the stanza. A variation containing six stanzas is called a double ballade.

baroque

a term used in literary criticism to describe literature that is complex or ornate in style or diction. Baroque works typically express tension, anxiety and violent emotion. The term 'Baroque Age' designates a period in Western European literature beginning in the late sixteenth century and ending about one hundred years later. Works of this period often mirror the qualities of works more generally associated with the label 'baroque' and sometimes feature elaborate conceits.

Examples of baroque works include John Lyly's 'Euphues: The Anatomy of Wit', Luis de Gongora's 'Soledads' and William Shakespeare's 'As You Like It'.

William Shakespeare

■ **baroque age**

see **baroque.**

■ **baroque period**

see **baroque.**

■ **Basho (1644-1694)**

Matsuo Basho was a Japanese poet, critic and essayist of the early Edo period. Basho is his literary name, which he derived from the plantain trees (basho) near a hut built for him by a disciple. Basho played a central role in the development of haiku. He composed stanzas of *haikai no renga* (a sequence of linked verses, usually by a group of poets), who's opening and most important stanza (hokku) was later separated as the verse form haiku. A master of hokku and the integration of verses in a sequence, Basho imbued what was a social pastime with the spirit of Zen and created a serious literary form capable of profound artistic expression. His poetry is noted for its sensitive exploration of nature of beauty, loneliness, suffering and death. Famous travel accounts are his own experiences of long and arduous journey. His masterpiece, *The Oku no hosomichi* (narrow road to the interior), is a reflection in poetry and prose on his travels through the northern hinterlands.

■ **bathos**

an unintentional shift from the sublime to the ridiculous, which can result from the use of overly elevated language to describe trivial subject matter, or from an exaggerated attempt at pathos which misfires to the point of being ludicrous. Bathos can be viewed as an unintentional anticlimax.

■ **Beat Generation**

see **Beat Movement.**

■ **Beat Movement**

a period featuring a group of American poets and novelists of the 1950s and 1960s — including Jack Kerouac, Allen Ginsberg, Gregory Corso, William S. Burroughs and Lawrence Ferlinghetti — who rejected established social and literary values. Using such techniques as stream of consciousness writing and jazz-influenced free verse and focusing on unusual or abnormal states of mind — generated by religious ecstasy or the use of drugs — the Beat writers aimed to create works that were unconventional in both form and subject matter.

Kerouac's 'On the Road' is perhaps the best-known example of a Beat Generation novel and Ginsberg's 'Howl' is a famous collection of Beat Poetry.

Allen Ginsberg

Beat Poets

see **Beat Movement.**

belles-lettres

a French term meaning 'fine letters' or 'beautiful writing'. It is often used as a synonym for literature, typically referring to imaginative and artistic rather than scientific or expository writing. Current usage sometimes restricts the meaning to light or humorous writing and appreciative essays about literature.

Lewis Carroll's 'Alice in Wonderland' epitomises the realm of belles-lettres.

Lewic Carroll

Ben Jonson (1572-1637)

Ben Jonson was an English dramatist and poet. His use of brilliant language and high- spirited buoyancy has earned him a reputation as one of the great playwrights in English literature. His first important play, *Every Man in His Humour*, was produced in 1598. It was followed by its companion piece, *Every Man out of His Humour* in 1599. In *The Poetaster* (1601) Jonson satirised several of his fellow playwrights. In 1604, he collaborated with Chapman and Marston on *the comedy Eastward Ho!* Production of *Volpone* in 1606 made him famous and rich. This was followed by his three other comic masterpieces, *Epicoene* (1609), *The Alchemist* (1610) and *Bartholomew Fair* (1614). He wrote two Roman tragedies, *Sejanus* (1603) and *Catiline* (1611). His good fortune declined with the failure of *The Devil Is an Ass* in 1616. His final plays were failures. Jonson's non-dramatic poetry includes *Epigrams* (1616), *The Forrest* (1616), notable for the two beautiful songs: *Drink to me only with thine eyes* and *Come, my Celia, let us prove* and *Underwoods* (1640). Jonson exerted a strong influence over his contemporaries.

Bertolt Brecht (1891-1956)

Bertolt Brecht was a German dramatist and poet. He was a controversial force in modern drama. His early plays show nihilistic expressionism like *Baal* (1919) and *Drums in the Night* (1922). He developed his so-called epic theatre with *Mann ist Mann* (1926) in which he used the technique of shock realisation in the spectator. He also created the distancing effect. Songs played an important part in his plays, they reveal Brecht's continued hostility towards the capitalist social structure as well as his bittersweet compassion for humanity. In 1933, Brecht went into exile under National Socialism, settling in Denmark and later in the United States. During his mature phase, he wrote *Mutter Courage und ihre Kinder* (*Mother Courage and her children*) (1941) and *Der gute Mensch von Sezuan* (*The Good Woman of Setzuan*, 1943), both concerned with ethical conduct. An outstanding example of epic theatre is *Der Kaukasische Kreidekreis*. Brecht lived in East Berlin after 1948 and directed the state-supported Berliner Ensemble.

■ bildungsroman

a German word meaning 'novel of development'. The bildungsroman is a study of the maturation of a youthful character, typically brought about through a series of social or sexual encounters that lead to self-awareness. Bildungsroman is used interchangeably with 'erziehungsro-man', a novel of initiation and education. When a bildungsroman is concerned with the development of an artist (as in James Joyce's 'A Portrait of the Artist as a Young Man'), it is often termed a 'kunstlerroman'.

Well-known bildungsroman include J. D. Salinger's 'The Catcher in the Rye', Robert Newton Peck's 'A Day No Pigs Would Die' and S. E. Hinton's 'The Outsiders'. Also known as Apprenticeship Novel, Coming of Age Novel, Erziehungsroman, or Kunstlerroman.

J. D. Salinger

■ biographical criticism

an approach to literature which suggests that knowledge of the author's life experiences can aid in the understanding of his or her work. While biographical information can sometimes complicate one's interpretation of a work and some formalist critics (such as the New Critics) disparage the use of the author's biography as a tool for textual interpretation, learning about the life of the author can often enrich a reader's appreciation for that author's work.

■ biography

a connected narrative that tells a person's life story. Biographies typically aim to be objective and closely detailed. James Boswell's 'The Life of Samuel Johnson' is a famous example of the form.

■ black aesthetic movement

a period of artistic and literary development among African

Americans in the 1960s and early 1970s. This was the first major African-American artistic movement since the Harlem Renaissance and was closely paralleled by the civil rights and black power movements. The black aesthetic writers attempted to produce works of art that would be meaningful to the black masses. Key figures in black aesthetics included one of its founders, poet and playwright Amiri Baraka, formerly known as LeRoi Jones; poet and essayist Haki R. Madhubuti, formerly Don L. Lee; poet and playwright Sonia Sanchez; and dramatist Ed Bullins.

Also known as Black Arts Movement.

■ black arts movement

see **black aesthetic movement.**

■ black comedy

see **black humour.**

■ black humour

writing that places grotesque elements side by side with humorous ones, in an attempt to shock the reader, forcing him or her to laugh at the horrifying reality of a disordered world.

Joseph Heller's novel 'Catch-22' is considered a superb example of the use of black humour. Other well-known authors who use black humour include Kurt Vonnegut, Edward Albee, Eugene Ionesco and Harold Pinter.

Also known as Black Comedy.

■ Black Mountain school

Black Mountain College and three of its instructors — Robert Creeley, Robert Duncan and Charles Olson — were all influential in projective verse, so poets working in projective verse are now referred as members of the Black Mountain school.

The 'Black Mountain Review' published much of the work of Black Mountain school poets.

Robert Creeley

■ blank verse

loosely, any unrhymed poetry, but more generally, unrhymed iambic pentameter verse (composed of lines of five two-syllable feet, with the first syllable accented, the second unaccented). Blank verse has been used by poets since the Renaissance for its flexibility and its graceful, dignified tone.

John Milton's 'Paradise Lost' is in blank verse, as are most of William Shakespeare's plays.

■ Bloomsbury Group

a group of English writers, artists and intellectuals who held informal artistic and philosophical discussions in Bloomsbury, a district of London, from around 1907 to the early 1930s. The Bloomsbury Group held no uniform philosophical beliefs but did commonly express an aversion to moral prudery and a desire for greater social tolerance.

At various times, the circle included Virginia Woolf, E. M. Forster, Clive Bell, Lytton Strachey and John Maynard Keynes.

■ bon mot

a French term meaning 'good word'. A bon mot is a witty remark or clever observation.

Charles Lamb and Oscar Wilde are celebrated for their witty bon mots. Two examples by Oscar Wilde stand out: (1) 'All women become their mothers. That is their tragedy. No man does. That's his'. (2) 'A man cannot be too careful in the choice of his enemies'.

■ bouts-rimes

an 18th century parlour game in which a list of rhyming words was drawn up and handed to the players, who had to make a poem from the list, keeping the rhymes in their original order.

■ breath verse

see **projective verse.**

■ broadside ballad

a ballad written in doggerel, printed on a single sheet of paper and sold for a penny or two on English street corners in the late 16th and early 17th centuries. The name of the tune to which they were to be sung was indicated on the sheet. The subject matter of broadside ballads covered a wide range of current, historical or simply curious events and also extended to moral exhortations and religious propaganda.

■ broken rhyme

a rhyme produced by dividing a word at the line break to make a rhyme with the end word of another line. Also called split rhyme

■ bucolic

derived from the Greek word for herdsman, an ancient term for a poem dealing with a pastoral subject.

■ burden

the central topic or principle idea, often repeated in a refrain.

■ burlesque

any literary work that uses exaggeration to make its subject appear ridiculous, either by treating a trivial subject with profound seriousness or by treating a dignified subject frivolously. The word 'burlesque' may also be used as an adjective, as in 'burlesque show', to mean 'striptease act'.

Examples of literary burlesque include the comedies of Aristophanes, Miguel de Cervantes's 'Don Quixote', Samuel Butler's poem 'Hudibras' and John Gay's play 'The Beggar's Opera'.

■ cacophony

discordant sounds in the jarring juxtaposition of harsh letters or syllables, sometimes inadvertent, but often deliberately used in poetry for effect, such as this line from John Updike's 'Player Piano': 'never my numb plunker fumbles'. Cacophony ('bad sound') may be unintentional in the writer's sense of music, or it may be used consciously for deliberate dramatic effect.

John Updike

■ cadence

the natural rhythm of language, caused by the alternation of accented and unaccented syllables. Much modern poetry— notably free v erse — deliberately manipulates cadence to create complex rhythmic effects. James Macpherson's 'Ossian poems' are richly cadenced, as is the poetry of the Symbolists, Walt Whitman and Amy Lowell.

Walt Whitman

■ caesura

a pause in a line of poetry, usually occurring near the middle. It typically corresponds to a break in the natural rhythm or sense of the line but is sometimes shifted to create special meanings or rhythmic effects. It may coincide with conventional punctuation marks, but not necessarily. A caesura within a line is indicated in scanning by the symbol (| |).

The opening line of Edgar Allan Poe's 'The Raven' contains a caesura following 'dreary': 'Once upon a midnight dreary, while I pondered weak and weary....'

■ canon

in a literary sense, the authoritative works of a particular writer; also, an accepted list of works perceived to represent a cultural, ideological, historical, or biblical grouping.

■ canto

a major division of a long or extended poem. A canto of a poem corresponds to a chapter of a novel.

■ canzone

a short Italian or Provencal lyric poem, commonly about love and often set to music. The 'canzone' has no set form but typically contains five or six stanzas made up of seven to twenty lines of eleven syllables each. A shorter, five- to ten-line 'envoy' or concluding stanza, completes the poem.

Masters of the 'canzone' form include Petrarch, Dante Alighieri,

Torquato Tasso and Guido Cavalcanti.

Dante Alighieri

■ carmina figurata/ figuratums

see **pattern poetry.**

■ carpe diem

a Latin term meaning 'seize the day'. This is a traditional theme of poetry, especially lyrics. A carpe diem poem advises the reader or the person it addresses to live for today and enjoy the pleasures of the moment.

Two celebrated carpe diem poems are Andrew Marvell's 'To His Coy Mistress' and Robert Herrick's poem beginning 'Gather ye rosebuds while ye may....'

■ catachresis

misuse or abuse of words; the use of the wrong word for the context, as atone for repent, ingenuous for ingenious, or a forced trope in which a word is used too far removed from its true meaning, as 'loud aroma' or 'velvet beautiful to the touch'.

■ catalectic/catalexis

metrically incomplete; the dropping of one or two unaccented syllables from the end of a line, thus ending with an incomplete foot.

■ catalog verse

a poem comprised of a list of persons, places, things, or abstract ideas which share a common denominator. An ancient form, it was originally a type of didactic poetry.

■ cataphora

the use of a grammatical substitute (like a pronoun) which has the same reference as the next word or phrase.

■ catharsis

meaning 'purgation', catharsis describes the release of the emotions of pity and fear by the audience at the end of a tragedy. In his 'Poetics', Aristotle discusses the importance of catharsis. The audience faces the misfortunes of the protagonist, which elicit pity and compassion. Simultaneously, the audience also confronts the failure of the protagonist, thus receiving a frightening reminder of human limitations and frailties. Ultimately, however, both these negative emotions are purged, because the tragic protagonist's suffering is an affirmation of human values rather than a despairing denial of them.

■ Catullus (84 B.C.-54 B.C.)

Caius Valerius Catullus known as Catullus, was a Roman poet and is considered the greatest writer of Latin lyric verse. He started writing in his early youth and was influenced by Callimachus and other Alexandrine and earlier Greek poets.

Catullus was particularly well known for his rude and crude poetry which, however finely polished, astonishes the reader with vitriolic obscenities and gross violations of good taste. Catullus was famous for his *Lesbia* poems. These poems express his deep passion and devotion and hatred and scorn for a mysterious lady. The mysterious lady has been identified as Lesbia. He also wrote long poems, the most notable among his long poems was *Attis* and he also wrote a nuptial poem honouring Thetis and Peleus and various short pieces. His satire is vigorous and flexible, his light poems joyful and full-bodied. Two of his most popular poems are the 10-line poem, touching and simple, which ends, *frater ave atque vale [hail, brother and farewell]* and *On the Death of Lesbia's Sparrow*. He was one of the Neoteric Poets.

■ Celtic Renaissance

a period of Irish literary and cultural history at the end of the nineteenth century. Followers of the movement aimed to create a romantic vision of Celtic myth and legend. The most significant works of the Celtic Renaissance typically present a dreamy, unreal world, usually in reaction against the reality of contemporary problems.

William Butler Yeats's 'The Wanderings of Oisin' is among the most significant works of the Celtic Renaissance.

Also known as Celtic Twilight.

■ Celtic Twilight

see **Celtic Renaissance.**

■ cento

poetry made up of lines borrowed from a combination of established authors, usually resulting in a change in meaning and a humorous effect.

■ chain rhyme

also called interlocking rhyme, a rhyme scheme in which a rhyme in a line of one stanza is used as a link to a rhyme in the next stanza, as in the aba bcb cdc, etc. of terza rima or the aaab cccb.

■ chain verse

similar to chain rhyme, but links words, phrases, or lines (instead of rhyme) by repeating them in succeeding stanzas, as in the pantoum, but there are many variations.

chanson de geste

literally, a song of heroic deeds, it refers to a class of Old French epic poems of the Middle Ages.

chant royal

an elaborate form of ballade in old French poetry, consisting of five stanzas of eleven lines, an envoi of eight lines and five rhymes. The rhyme scheme is usually ababccddede.

chapbook

a small book or pamphlet containing ballads, poems, popular tales or tracts, etc.

character

broadly speaking, a person in a literary work. The actions of characters are what constitute the plot of a story, novel, or poem. There are numerous types of characters, ranging from simple, stereotypical figures to intricate, multifaceted ones. In the techniques of Anthropomorphism and personification, animals — and even places or things — can assume aspects of character. 'Characterisation' is the process by which an author creates vivid, believable characters in a work of art. This may be done in a variety of ways, including (1) direct description of the character by the narrator; (2) the direct presentation of the speech, thoughts, or actions of the character; and (3) the responses of other characters to the character. The term 'character' also refers to a form originated by the ancient Greek writer Theophrastus that later became popular in the seventeenth and eighteenth centuries. It is a short essay or sketch of a person who prominently displays a specific attribute or quality, such as miserliness or ambition.

Notable characters in literature include Oedipus Rex, Don Quixote de la Mancha, Macbeth, Candide, Hester Prynne, Ebenezer Scrooge, Huckleberry Finn, Jay Gatsby, Scarlett O'Hara, James Bond and Kunta Kinte.

characterisation

see **character.**

Charles Dickens (1812–70)

Charles Dickens is a famous English author. He was born in Portsmouth. He is one of the worlds most popular, creative and skilled novelists.

His early childhood was spent in London and in Chatham. When he was 12, his father was imprisoned for debt and Charles was compelled to work in a blacking warehouse. At the age of 17, he became a court stenographer. Later, he was an expert parliamentary reporter for the Morning Chronicle. His sketches, mostly of London life (signed Boz), began appearing in periodicals in 1833 and the collection *Sketches by Boz* (1836) was a success. Dickens worked vigorously for his readers, producing novels that appeared first in monthly instalments and then were made into books. The book, *Oliver Twist* was followed by *Nicholas Nickleby* (1839).

Dombey and Son (1848) was the first in a string of triumphant novels including *David Copperfield* (1850), his own favourite novel, which was partly autobiographical, *Hard Times* (1854), *Little Dorrit* (1857), *A Tale of Two Cities* (1859) and *Great Expectations* (1861).

Exhausted from the tours of platform readings, his health broke and in 1970. He died leaving his last novel, *The Mystery of Edwin Drood*, unfinished.

chaucerian stanza

see **rhyme royal.**

chiasmus

an inverted parallelism; the reversal of the order of corresponding words or phrases (with or without exact repetition) in successive clauses, which are usually parallel in syntax.

Chinua Achebe (1930–)

Achebe was a Nigerian writer. He graduated from the University College at Ibadan (1953). Achebe is one of Africa's most acclaimed authors and considered by some to be the father of modern African literature. His early novels, including the groundbreaking *Things Fall Apart* (1958)—probably the most widely read book by a black African writer and *No Longer at Ease* (1960), describe poignantly the effects of European colonialism on Igbo society, Nigeria and newly independent African nations. He also served as a diplomat (1966–68) for Biafra during the Nigerian civil war and later wrote two volumes of poetry, *Beware, Soul Brother* (1971) and *Christmas in Biafra* (1973) and one of literary essays, *Morning Yet on Creation Day* (1975), about the war. He was a teacher at the University of Nigeria, Nsukka (1976–81) and was the founding editor (1971) of the influential journal *Okike*. He has also written numerous short stories, children's books and a book of essays, *Home and Exile* (2000).

choriamb

in ancient poetry, a metrical foot consisting of four syllables, the first two forming a trochee and the second two an iambus.

choric ode

see **pindaric verse.**

chorus

in ancient Greek drama, a group of actors who commented on and interpreted the unfolding action on the stage. Initially, the chorus was a major component of the presentation, but over time, it became less significant, with its numbers reduced and its role eventually limited to commentary between acts. By the sixteenth century, the chorus — if employed at all — was typically a single person who provided a prologue and an epilogue and occasionally appeared between acts to introduce or underscore an important event.

The chorus in William Shakespeare's 'Henry V' functions in this way. Modern dramas rarely feature a chorus, but T. S.

Eliot's 'Murder in the Cathedral' and Arthur Miller's 'A View from the Bridge' are notable exceptions. The stage manager in Thornton Wilder's 'Our Town' performs a role similar to that of the chorus.

T. S. Elliot

■ Christopher Marlowe (1564-1593)

Christopher Marlowe was an English dramatist and poet. Before Shakespeare, he was considered the greatest English dramatist. In 1587, he went to London and became an actor and dramatist for the Lord Admiral's Company. Some of his most important plays are the two parts of *Tamburlaine the Great* (1587), *Dr. Faustus* (588), *The Jew of Malta* (589) and *Edward II* (592). His plays centre on a great personality who is destroyed by his own passion and ambition. Marlowe's plays are never merely sensational, though they are filled with violence, brutality, passion and bloodshed. His plays are raised to high level because Marlowe uses poetic beauty and dignity of language. His influences can be seen in Shakespeare canon like in King Henry VI. His best non-dramatic long poem is *Hero and Leander*, which were published in 1598.

■ chronicle

a record of events presented in chronological order. Although the scope and level of detail provided varies greatly among the chronicles surviving from ancient times, some, such as the 'Anglo-Saxon Chronicle', feature vivid descriptions and a lively recounting of events. During the Elizabethan Age, many dramas — appropriately called 'chronicle plays' — were based on material from chronicles.

Many of William Shakespeare's dramas of English history as well

Christopher Marlowe

as Christopher Marlowe's 'Edward II' are based in part on Raphael Holinshead's 'Chronicles of England, Scotland and Ireland'.

■ chronology

the cause and effect sequence of events.

cinquain

a five-line stanza of syllabic verse, the successive lines containing two, four, six, eight and two syllables. The cinquain, based on the Japanese 'haiku', was an innovation of the American poet, Adelaide Crapsey.

classical

in its strictest definition in literary criticism, classicism refers to works of ancient Greek or Roman literature. The term may also be used to describe a literary work of recognised importance (a 'classic') from any time period or literature that exhibits the traits of classicism.

Classical authors from ancient Greek and Roman times include Juvenal and Homer. Examples of later works and authors now described as classical include French

James Fenimore Cooper

literature of the seventeenth century, Western novels of the nineteenth century and American fiction of the mid-nineteenth century such as that written by James Fenimore Cooper and Mark Twain.

classicism

a term used in literary criticism to describe critical doctrines that have their roots in ancient Greek and Roman literature, philosophy and art. Works associated with classicism typically exhibit restraint on the part of the author, unity of design and purpose, clarity, simplicity, logical organisation and respect for tradition.

Examples of literary classicism include Cicero's prose, the dramas of Pierre Corneille and Jean Racine, the Poetry of John Dryden and Alexander Pope and the writings of J. W. von Goethe, G. E. Lessing and T. S. Eliot.

G. E. Lessing

clerihew

a comic light verse, two couplets in length, rhyming aabb, usually dealing with a person mentioned in the initial rhyme.

cliché

an idea or expression that has become tired and trite from overuse, its freshness and clarity having worn off. Clichés often take the essence out of the sentence and are usually a sign of weak writing.

■ climax

1. the turning point in a narrative, the moment when the conflict is at its most intense. Typically, the structure of stories, novels and plays is one of rising action, in which tension builds to the climax, followed by falling action, in which tension lessens as the story moves to its conclusion.

The climax in James Fenimore Cooper's 'The Last of the Mohicans' occurs when Magua and his captive Cora are pursued to the edge of a cliff by Uncas. Magua kills Uncas but is subsequently killed by Hawkeye.

2. rhetorically, a series of words, phrases, or sentences arranged in a continuously ascending order of intensity. If the ascending order is not maintained, an anticlimax or bathos results.

■ close reading

interpretation begins with close reading. In this process, you note specific uses of language, such as imagery, symbols, repeated terms, patterns of expression, the tone of the speaker and the main ideas (themes) the writer introduces. Whether close reading takes the form of writing, discussion, or silent observation, it should be based on a careful questioning of the text.

■ close rhyme

a rhyme of two contiguous or close words, such as in the idiomatic expressions, 'true blue' or 'fair and square'.

■ closed couplet

a couplet in which the sense and syntax is self-contained within its two lines, as opposed to an open couplet.

■ closet drama

a literary work written in the form of a drama, but intended by the author only for reading, not for performance in the theatre.

■ closure

the effect of finality, balance and completeness which leaves the reader with a sense of fulfilled expectations. Though the term is sometimes employed to describe the effects of individual repetitive elements, such as rhyme, metrical patterns, parallelism, refrains and stanzas, its most significant application is in reference to the concluding portion of the entire poem.

■ colloquial

refers to a type of informal diction that reflects casual, conversational language and often includes slang expressions.

■ colloquialism

a word, phrase, or form of pronunciation that is acceptable in casual conversation but not in formal, written communication. It is considered more acceptable than slang.

Rudyard Kipling's

An example of colloquialism can be found in Rudyard Kipling's 'Barrack-room Ballads':

When 'Omer smote 'is bloomin' lyre
He'd 'eard men sing by land and sea;
An' what he thought 'e might require
'E went an' took — the same as me!

comedy

one of two major types of drama, the other being tragedy. Its aim is to amuse and it typically ends happily. Comedy assumes many forms, such as farce and burlesque and uses a variety of techniques, from parody to satire. In a restricted sense, the term comedy refers only to dramatic presentations, but in general usage, it is commonly applied to non-dramatic works as well.

Examples of comedies range from the plays of Aristophanes, Terrence and Plautus, Dante Alighieri's 'The Divine Comedy', Francois Rabelais's 'Pantagruel' and 'Gargantua' and some of Geoffrey Chaucer's tales and William Shakespeare's plays to Noel Coward's play 'Private Lives' and James Thurber's short story 'The Secret Life of Walter Mitty'.

Geoffrey Chaucer

comedy of manners

a play about the manners and conventions of an aristocratic, highly sophisticated society. The characters are usually types rather than individualised personalities and the plot is less important than the atmosphere. Such plays were an important aspect of late seventeenth-century English comedy. The comedy of manners was revived in the eighteenth century by Oliver Goldsmith and Richard Brinsley Sheridan, enjoyed a second revival in the late nineteenth century and has endured into the twentieth century.

Examples of comedies of manners include William Congreve's 'The Way of the World' in the late seventeenth century, Oliver Goldsmith's 'She Stoops to Conquer' and Richard Brinsley Sheridan's 'The School for Scandal' in the eighteenth century, Oscar Wilde's 'The Importance of Being Earnest' in the nineteenth century and W. Somerset Maugham's 'The Circle' in the twentieth century.

William Congreve

comic relief

the use of humour to lighten the mood of a serious or tragic story, especially in plays. The technique is very common in Elizabethan works and can be an integral part of the plot or simply a brief event designed to break the tension of the scene.

The Gravediggers' scene in William Shakespeare's 'Hamlet' is a frequently cited example of comic relief.

coming of age novel

see **bildungsroman.**

commedia dell'arte

an Italian term meaning 'the comedy of guilds' or 'the comedy of professional actors'. This form of dramatic comedy was popular in Italy during the sixteenth century. Actors were assigned stock roles (such as Pulcinella, the stupid servant, or Pantalone, the old merchant) and given a basic plot to follow, but all dialogue was improvised. The roles were rigidly typed and the plots were formulaic, usually revolving around young lovers who thwarted their elders and attained wealth and happiness. A rigid convention of the commedia dell'arte is the periodic intrusion of Harlequin, who interrupts the play with low buffoonery.

Peppino de Filippo's 'Metamorphoses of a Wandering Minstrel' gave modern audiences an idea of what commedia dell'arte may have been like. Various scenarios for commedia dell'arte were compiled in Petraccone's La commedia dell'arte, storia, technica, scenari, published in 1927.

common measure

a meter consisting chiefly of seven iambi feet arranged in rhymed pairs, thus a line with four accents followed by a line with three accents, usually in a four-line stanza. It is also called common meter.

companion poem

a poem that is associated with another, which it complements.

complaint

a lyric poem, popular in the Renaissance, in which the speaker expresses sorrow about his or her condition. Typically, the speaker's sadness is caused by an unresponsive lover, but some complaints cite other sources of unhappiness, such as poverty or fate.

A commonly cited example is 'A Complaint by Night of the Lover Not Beloved' by Henry Howard, Earl of Surrey. Thomas Sackville's 'Complaint of Henry, Duke of Buckingham' traces the duke's unhappiness to his ruthless ambition.

Thomas Sackville'

■ conceit

a clever and fanciful metaphor, usually expressed through elaborate and extended comparison that presents a striking parallel between two seemingly dissimilar things — for example, elaborately comparing a beautiful woman to an object like a garden or the sun. The conceit was a popular device throughout the Elizabethan Age and Baroque Age and was the principal technique of the seventeenth-century English metaphysical poets. This usage of the word conceit is unrelated to the best-known definition of conceit as an

Emily Dickinson

arrogant attitude or behaviour. The conceit figures prominently in the works of John Donne, Emily Dickinson and T. S. Eliot.

■ concrete

it is the opposite of abstract and refers to a thing that actually exists or a description that allows the reader to experience an object or concept with the senses. Henry David Thoreau's 'Walden' contains much concrete description of nature and wildlife.

Henry David Thoreau

■ concrete poetry

poetry in which visual elements play a large part in the poetic effect. Punctuation marks, letters, or words are arranged on a page to form a visual design: a cross, for example, or a bumblebee.

Max Bill and Eugene Gomringer were among the early practitioners of concrete poetry; Haroldo de Campos and Augusto de Campos are among contemporary authors of concrete poetry.

■ confession

autobiography regarded as a form of prose fiction, or prose fiction cast in the form of autobiography.

■ confessional poetry

a form of poetry in which the poet reveals very personal, intimate, sometimes shocking information about himself or herself.

Anne Sexton, Sylvia Plath, Robert Lowell and John Berryman wrote poetry in the confessional vein.

Robert Lowell

■ conflict

the conflict in a work of fiction is the issue to be resolved in the story. It usually occurs between two characters, the protagonist and the antagonist, or between the protagonist and society or the protagonist and himself or herself.

Conflict in Theodore Dreiser's novel 'Sister Carrie' comes as a result of urban society, while Jack London's short story 'To Build a Fire' concerns the protagonist's battle against the cold and himself.

■ connotation

the impression that a word gives beyond its defined meaning. Connotations may be universally understood or may be significant only to a certain group.

Both 'horse' and 'steed' denote the same animal, but 'steed' has a different connotation, deriving from the chivalrous or romantic narratives in which the word was once often used.

■ connotation

1. the suggestion of a meaning by a word beyond what it explicitly denotes or describes. The word, 'home', for example, means the place where one lives, but by connotation, also suggests security, family, love and comfort.

2. consonance occurs in poetry when words appearing at the ends of two or more verses have similar final consonant sounds but have final vowel sounds that differ, as with 'stuff' and 'off'.

Consonance is found in 'The curfew tolls the knells of parting day' from Thomas Grey's 'An Elegy Written in a Country Church Yard'.

Also known as Half Rhyme or Slant Rhyme.

■ Conrad Aiken (1889-1973)

Conrad Aiken was an American author who graduated from Harvard in 1912. He is best known for his poetry. They are preoccupied with the sound and structure of music. His volumes of verse include *The Charnel Rose* (1918), *Selected Poems* won the Pulitzer Prize in 1929, *Brownstone Eclogues* (1942), *Collected Poems* (1953), *A Letter from Li Po* (1956), *A Seizure of Limericks* (1964) and *The Clerk's Journal* (1971). Emily Dickinson's reputation as a literary figure was established in 1924 when Conard edited her book *Selected Poems.* In *Blue Voyage* (1927) and *Great Circle* (1933), his interest in psychopathology is evident. His collected critical essays, *A Reviewer's ABC* appeared in 1958. *Mr. Arcularis* and *Silent Snow, Secret Snow* are some of his short stories. Aiken held (1950–57) the poetry chair at the Library of Congress and was awarded with the National Medal for Literature in 1969.

■ content

the substance of a poem; the impressions, facts and ideas it contains—the 'what-is-being-said'.

■ contextual symbol

see **symbol.**

■ controlling metaphor

a symbolic story, where the whole poem may be a metaphor for something else.

■ conventions

in a literary sense, established 'codes' of basic principles and procedures for types of works that are recurrent in literature. The prevailing conventions of their time strongly influence writers to select content, forms, style, diction, etc., which is acceptable to the cultural expectations of the public.

■ corrido

a Mexican ballad. Examples of corridos include 'Muerte del afamado Bilito', 'La voz de mi conciencia', 'Lucio Perez', 'La juida' and 'Los presos'.

■ cosmic irony

see **irony.**

■ couplet

two successive lines of poetry, usually of equal length and rhythmic correspondence, with end-words that rhyme. The couplet, for practical purposes, is the shortest stanza form, but is frequently joined with other couplets to form a poem with no stanzaic divisions.

■ courtly love

a late medieval idealised convention, establishing a code for the conduct of amorous affairs of ladies and their lovers. Expressed and spread by the minnesingers and troubadours, it became associated with the literary concept of love until the 19th century.

■ crambo

a game in which one player gives a word or line of verse to be matched in rhyme by the other players.

■ **cretic**

used in ancient poetry, a metrical foot consisting of a short syllable between two long syllables, as in thirty-nine.

■ **crime literature**

a genre of fiction that focuses on the environment, behaviour and psychology of criminals.

Prominent writers of crime novels include John Wainwright, Colin Watson, Nicolas Freeling,

Ruth Rendell

Ruth Rendell, Jessica Mann, Mickey Spillane and Patricia Highsmith.

■ **crisis**

a turning point in the action of a story that has a powerful effect on the protagonist. Opposing forces come together decisively to lead to the climax of the plot.

■ **criticaster**

an inferior or petty critic.

■ **criticism**

the systematic study and evaluation of literary works, usually based on a specific method or set of principles. An important part of literary studies since ancient times, the practice of criticism has given rise to numerous theories, methods and 'schools', sometimes producing conflicting, even contradictory, interpretations of literature in general as well as of individual works. Even such basic issues as what constitutes a poem or a novel have been the subject of much criticism over the centuries. Seminal texts of literary criticism include Plato's 'Republic', Aristotle's 'Poetics', Sir Philip

Sir Philip Sidney

Sidney's 'The Defence of Poesie', John Dryden's 'Of Dramatic Poesie' and William Wordsworth's 'Preface' to the second edition of his Lyrical Ballads. Contemporary schools of criticism include deconstruction, feminist, psychoanalytic, poststructuralist, new historicist, postcolonialist and reader-response.

William Wordsworth

■ **cross rhyme**

a rhyme scheme of abab, also called alternate rhyme. The term derives from long-line verse such as hexameter, in which two lines have caesural words rhymed together and end words rhymed together, as in Swinburne's.

■ **cultural criticism**

an approach to literature that focuses on the historical as well as social, political and economic contexts of a work. Popular culture—mass-produced and consumed cultural artefacts ranging from advertising to popular fiction to television to rock music—is given equal emphasis as 'high culture'. Cultural critics use widely eclectic strategies such as new historicism, psychology, gender studies and deconstructionist to analyse not only literary texts but also everything from radio talk shows, comic strips, calendar art, commercials, to travel guides and baseball cards.

■ **cycle**

the aggregate of accumulated literature, plays or musical works treating the same theme. In poetry, the term is typically applied to epic or narrative poems about a mythical or heroic event or character.

■ **D.H. Lawrence (1885-1930)**

David Herbert Lawrence was an English novelist and poet. He ranked among the most influential and controversial literary figures of the 20th century. His novels were misunderstood and were even attacked and suppressed because of their frank treatment of sexual matters.

Lawrence was on born on September 11, 1885, in Eastwood, Nottinghamshire, to a coal miner. His mother was a schoolteacher. The disparity in social status between his parents was a recurrent motif in Lawrence's fiction. In 1908, he graduated from University College, Nottingham. Lawrence published his first poems in the English Review in 1909 and his first novel, *The White Peacock*, in 1911. His early fiction, *Sons and Lovers* (1913), deals with life in a mining town.

The Rainbow (1915) and *Women in Love* (1921), perhaps his best novels, explore with outspoken candour the sexual and psychological relationships of men and women. His most original poetry, published in Birds, Beasts and Flowers (1923), flowed from his experience of nature in the south western United States and the Mediterranean region.

From 1926, Lawrence lived chiefly in Italy, where he wrote and rewrote his most notorious novel, *Lady Chatterley's Lover* (1928), which deals with the sexually fulfilling love affair between a member of the nobility and her husband's gamekeeper. In 1932, its expurgated version was published. In March 2, 1930, in a sanatorium in Vence, France Lawrence died.

■ **dactyl**

see **foot.**

dactyl or dactylic

a metrical foot of three syllables, the first of which is long or accented and the next two short or unaccented.

dactylic meter

see **foot.**

dadaism

a protest movement in art and literature founded by Tristan Tzara in 1916. Followers of the movement expressed their outrage at the destruction brought about by World War I by revolting against numerous forms of social convention. The Dadaists presented works marked by calculated madness and flamboyant nonsense. They stressed total freedom of expression, commonly through primitive displays of emotion and illogical, often senseless, poetry. The movement ended shortly after the war, when it was replaced by surrealism.

Proponents of Dadaism include Andre Breton, Louis Aragon, Philippe Soupault and Paul Eluard.

Daniel Defoe or De Foe (1660 –1731)

He was an English writer and was born in London. Being educated at a Dissenters' academy, he was self-reliant, industrious, possessing a strong notion of personal and moral responsibility. Although intended for the Presbyterian ministry, he had by 1683 set himself up as a merchant dealing in many different commodities. In 1962, Defoe went bankrupt. Defoe's first important publication was *An Essay upon Projects* (1698), but he received real fame from the poem *The True-born Englishman* (1701). He got imprisoned for *Queen Anne's reign* and *The Shortest Way with Dissenters* (1702), an ironic defence of High Church animosity against nonconformists. He was rescued by Robert Harley and subsequently served the statesman as a political agent.

He is also known as the father of modern journalism. During his lifetime, he was associated with 26 periodicals. He was nearly sixty when he turned to writing novels. In 1719, he published his famous *Life and Strange Surprising Adventures of Robinson Crusoe.* Based in part on the experiences of Alexander Selkirk, Robinson Crusoe describes the daily life of a man marooned on a desert island. Two excellent examples of his semi historical recreations are the *Moll Flanders* (1722) and an account of the 1665 great plague in London, entitled *A Journal of the Plague Year* (1722).

Dante Gabriel Rossetti (1828-1882)

Dante Gabriel Rossetti, an English poet and painter, was the founder of the Pre-Raphaelites. To spread the ideas, he along with his group published, in 1850, a short-lived magazine, the *Germ.* Dante's best poem *The Blessed*

Damozel was published in this magazine when he was only 19 years old. The first edition of his collected works appeared in 1870. Although he began his career as a painter, Rossetti's lasting reputation rests upon his poetry. His poetry is noted for its pictorial effects and its atmosphere of luxurious beauty. He was a master of the sonnet form and his sonnet sequence *The House of Life* is one of his finest works. His other notable works include the ballad *Sister Helen* and the dramatic monologues *Jenny* and *A Last Confession*. His translations from the Italian appeared as *Dante and His Circle* (1861).

■ decadents

the followers of a nineteenth-century literary movement that had its beginnings in French Aestheticism. Decadent literature displays a fascination with perverse and morbid states; a search for novelty and sensation — the 'new thrill'; a preoccupation with mysticism; and a belief in the senselessness of human existence. The movement is closely associated with the doctrine Art for Art's Sake. The term 'decadence' is sometimes used to denote a decline in the quality of art or literature following a period of greatness.

Major French decadents are Charles Baudelaire and Arthur Rimbaud. English decadents include Oscar Wilde, Ernest Dowson and Frank Harris.

Ernest Dowson

■ decameter

a line of verse consisting of ten metrical feet.

■ decasyllable

a metrical line of ten syllables or a poem composed of ten-syllable lines.

■ deconstruction

a method of literary criticism developed by Jacques Derrida and characterised by multiple conflicting interpretations of a given work. Deconstructionists consider the impact of the language of a work and suggest that the true meaning of the work is not necessarily the meaning that the author intended.

Jacques Derrida's 'De la grammatologie' is the seminal text on deconstructive strategies; among American practitioners of this method of criticism are Paul de Man and J. Hillis Miller.

■ decorum

in literary parlance, the appropriateness of a work to its subject, its genre and its audience.

■ deduction

the process of reaching a conclusion through reasoning, from general premises to a specific premise.

An example of deduction is present in the following syllogism:

Premise: All mammals are animals.

Premise: All whales are mammals.

Conclusion: Therefore, all whales are animals.

■ denotation

the definition of a word, apart from the impressions or feelings it creates in the reader.

The word 'apartheid' denotes a political and economic policy of segregation by race, but its connotations — oppression, slavery, inequality — are numerous.

■ denouement

a French word meaning 'the unknotting'. In literary criticism, it denotes the resolution of conflict in fiction or drama. The denouement follows the climax and provides an outcome to the primary plot situation as well as an explanation of secondary plot complications. The denouement often involves a character's recognition of his or her state of mind or moral condition.

A well-known example of denouement is the last scene of the play 'As You Like It' by William Shakespeare, in which couples are married, an evildoer repents, the identities of two disguised characters are revealed and a ruler is restored to power. Also known as Falling Action.

■ description

descriptive writing is intended to allow a reader to picture the scene or setting in which the action of a story takes place. The form this description takes often evokes an intended emotional response — a dark, spooky graveyard will evoke fear and a peaceful, sunny meadow will evoke calmness.

An example of a descriptive story is Edgar Allan Poe's 'Landor's Cottage', which offers a detailed depiction of a New York country estate.

■ detective story

a narrative about the solution of a mystery or the identification of a criminal. The conventions of the detective story include the detective's scrupulous use of logic in solving the mystery; incompetent or ineffectual police; a suspect who appears guilty at first but is later proved innocent; and the detective's friend or confidant — often the narrator — whose slowness in interpreting clues emphasises, by contrast, the detective's brilliance.

Edgar Allan Poe's 'Murders in the Rue Morgue' is commonly regarded as the earliest example of this type of story. With this work, Poe established many of the conventions of the detective story genre, which are still in practice. Other practitioners of this vast and extremely popular genre include Arthur Conan Doyle, Dashiell Hammett and Agatha Christie.

■ deus ex machina

a Latin term meaning 'god out of a machine'. In Greek drama, a god was often lowered onto the stage by a mechanism of some kind to rescue the hero or untangle the plot. By extension, the term refers to any artificial device or coincidence used to bring about a convenient and simple solution to a plot. This is a common device in melodramas and includes such fortunate circumstances as the sudden receipt of a legacy to save the family farm or a last-minute stay of execution. The deus ex machina invariably rewards the virtuous and punishes evildoers.

Examples of deus ex machina include King Louis XIV in Jean-Baptiste Moliere's 'Tartuffe' and Queen Victoria in 'The Pirates of Penzance' by William Gilbert and Arthur Sullivan. Bertolt Brecht parodies the abuse of such devices in the conclusion of his 'Threepenny Opera'.

■ diacope

see **epizeuxis.**

■ diaeresis or dieresis

the pronunciation of two adjacent vowels as separate sounds rather than as a dipthong, as in coordinate; also, the mark indicating the separate pronunciation, as in naïve.

■ dialect

a type of informational diction. Dialects are spoken by definable groups of people from a particular geographic region, economic group, or social class. Writers use dialect to contrast and express differences in educational, class, social and regional backgrounds of their characters.

■ dialogue

in its widest sense, dialogue is simply conversation between people in a literary work; in its most restricted sense, it refers specifically to the speech of characters in a drama. As a specific literary genre, a 'dialogue' is a composition in which characters debate an issue or idea.

The Greek philosopher Plato frequently expounded his theories in the form of dialogues.

■ diary

a personal written record of daily events and thoughts. As private documents, diaries are supposedly not intended for an audience, but some, such as those of Samuel Pepys and Anais Nin, are known for their high literary quality.

'The Diary of Anne Frank' is an example of a well-known diary discovered and published after the author's death. Many writers have used the diary form as a deliberate literary device, as in Nikolai Gogol's story 'Diary of a Madman'.

Nikolai Gogol

■ **dibrach**

see **pyrrhic.**

■ **diction**

the selection and arrangement of words in a literary work. Either or both may vary depending on the desired effect. There are four general types of diction: 'formal', used in scholarly or lofty writing; 'informal', used in relaxed but educated conversation; 'colloquial', used in everyday speech; and 'slang', containing newly coined words and other terms not accepted in formal usage.

■ **didactic**

a term used to describe works of literature that aim to teach some moral, religious, political, or practical lesson. Although didactic elements are often found in artistically pleasing works, the term 'didactic' usually refers to literature in which the message is more important than the form. The term may also be used to criticise a work that the critic finds 'overly didactic', that is, heavy-handed in its delivery of a lesson.

Examples of didactic literature include John Bunyan's 'Pilgrim's Progress', Alexander Pope's 'essay on Criticism', Jean-Jacques Rousseau's 'Emile' and Elizabeth Inchbald's 'Simple Story'.

■ **didactic poetry**

poetry which is clearly intended for the purpose of instruction — to impart theoretical, moral, or practical knowledge, or to explain the principles of some art or science.

■ **diiamb or diamb**

in ancient poetry, a metrical foot consisting of four syllables, with the first and third short and the second and fourth long, i.e., two iambs considered as a single foot.

■ **dimeter**

a line of verse consisting of two metrical feet, or of two dipodies.

■ **dionysian**

see **Apollonian and Dionysian.**

■ **diphthong**

the sound formed by two merged vowels, highly prevalent in English, e.g. the vowel sounds of 'loud', 'new', 'why'.

■ **dipody or dipodic verse**

a double foot; a unit of two feet.

■ **dirge**

a poem of grief or lamentation, especially one intended to accompany funeral or memorial rites.

discordia concours

a Latin phrase meaning 'discord in harmony'. The term was coined by the eighteenth-century English writer Samuel Johnson to describe 'a combination of dissimilar images or discovery of occult resemblances in things apparently unlike'. Johnson created the expression by reversing a phrase by the Latin poet Horace.

The metaphysical poetry of John Donne, Richard Crashaw, Abraham Cowley, George Herbert and Edward Taylor among others, contains many examples of discordia concours. In Donne's 'A Valediction: Forbidding Mourning', the poet compares the union of himself with his lover to a draftsman's compass: If they be two, they are two so, As stiff twin compasses are two: Thy soul, the fixed foot, makes no show

To move, but doth, if the other do; And though it in the center sit, Yet when the other far doth roam, It leans and hearkens after it and grows erect, as that comes home.

Abraham Cowley

displacement

the adaptation of myth and metaphor to canons of morality or plausibility.

dispondee

in ancient poetry, a metrical foot consisting of four long syllables, equivalent to a double spondee.

dissonance

a combination of harsh or jarring sounds, especially in poetry. Although such combinations may be accidental, poets sometimes intentionally make them to achieve particular effects. Dissonance is also sometimes used to refer to close but not identical rhymes. When this is the case, the word functions as a synonym for consonance.

Robert Browning, Gerard Manley Hopkins and many other poets have made deliberate use of dissonance.

Gerard Manley Hopkins

■ **distich**

a strophic unit of two lines; a pair of poetic lines or verses which together comprise a complete sense.

■ **disyllabic rhyme**

a rhyme in which two final syllables of words have the same sound.

■ **disyllable**

a word of two syllables.

■ **dithyramb**

in classic poetry, a type of melic verse associated with drunken revelry and performed to honour Dionysus (Bacchus), the Greek god of wine and ecstasy. In modern usage, the term has come to mean a poem of impassioned frenzy and irregular character.

■ **ditty**

a little poem meant to be sung.

■ **dochmius or dochmii**

in ancient Greek prosody, a metrical foot consisting of five syllables, the first and fourth being short and the second, third and fifth long.

■ **documentary**

a work that features a large amount of documentary material such as newspaper stories, trial transcripts and legal reports. Such works can include fictionalised segments or may contain a fictional story in which the author incorporates real-life information or events; these are referred to as documentary novels. Examples of documentary novels include the works of Theodore Dreiser, Emile Zola, John Dos Passos and James T. Farrell. An example of a non-fictional literary documentary is James Agee's and Walker Evans's 'Let Us Now Praise Famous Men'.

Emile Zola

■ **documentary novel**

see **documentary.**

■ **dodecasyllable**

a metrical line of twelve syllables.

■ **doggerel**

originally applied to poetry of loose irregular measure, it now is used to describe crudely written poetry which lacks artistry in form or meaning.

■ **doppelganger**

a literary technique by which a character is duplicated (usually in the form of an alter ego, though sometimes as a ghostly counterpart) or divided into two distinct, usually opposite personalities. The use of this character device is widespread in nineteenth- and twentieth-century literature and indicates a growing awareness among authors that the 'self' is really a composite of many 'selves'.

A well-known story containing a doppelganger character is Robert Louis Stevenson's 'Dr. Jekyll and Mr. Hyde', which dramatises an internal struggle between good and evil. Also known as The Double.

■ dorian ode

see **pindaric verse.**

■ double dactyl

a word with two dactyls, such as counterintelligence or parliamentarian; also, a modern form of light verse consisting of two quatrains with two dactyls per line. The first line is a hyphenated nonsense word, often 'higgledy-piggledy'; the second line is a proper name and the sixth line is a single double dactyl word. The fourth and eighth lines are truncated, lacking the final two unaccented syllables and rhyme with each other.

■ double entendre

a corruption of a French phrase meaning 'double meaning'. The term is used to indicate a word or phrase that is deliberately ambiguous, especially when one of the meanings is risqué or improper.

An example of a double entendre is the Elizabethan usage of the verb 'die', which refers both to death and to orgasm.

■ draft

any preliminary version of a written work. An author may write dozens of drafts, which are revised to form the final work, or he or she may write only one, with few or no revisions.

Dorothy Parker's observation that 'I can't write five words but that I change seven' humorously indicates the purpose of the draft.

■ drama

in its widest sense, a drama is any work designed to be presented by actors on a stage. Similarly, 'drama' denotes a broad literary genre that includes a variety of forms, from pageant and spectacle to tragedy and comedy, as well as countless types and subtypes. More commonly, in modern usage, however, a drama is a work that treats serious subjects and themes but does not aim at the grandeur of tragedy. This use of the term originated with the eighteenth-century French writer Denis Diderot, who used the word drame to designate his plays about middle-class life; thus 'drama' typically features characters of a less exalted stature than those of tragedy.

Examples of classical dramas include Menander's comedy 'Dyscolus' and Sophocles' tragedy and 'Oedipus Rex'. Contemporary dramas include Eugene O'Neill's 'The Iceman Cometh', Lillian Hellman's 'Little Foxes' and August Wilson's 'Ma' Rainey's Black Bottom'.

Denis Diderot

■ **dramatic irony**

occurs when the audience of a play or the reader of a work of literature knows something that a character in the work itself does not know. The irony is in the contrast between the intended meaning of the statements or actions of a character and the additional information understood by the audience.

A celebrated example of dramatic irony is in Act V of William Shakespeare's 'Romeo and Juliet', where two young lovers meet their end as a result of a tragic misunderstanding. Here, the audience has full knowledge that Juliet's apparent 'death' is merely temporary; she will regain her senses when the mysterious 'sleeping potion' she has taken wears off. But Romeo, mistaking Juliet's drug-induced trance for true death, kills himself in grief. Upon awakening, Juliet discovers Romeo's corpse and, in despair, slays herself.

■ **dramatic monologue**

a literary work which consists of a revealing one-way conversation by a character or persona, usually directed to a second person or to an imaginary audience. It typically involves a critical moment of a specific situation, with the speaker's words unintentionally providing a revelation of his character.

■ **dramatic poetry**

any lyric work that employs elements of drama such as dialogue, conflict, or characterisation, but excluding works that are intended for stage presentation. A monologue is a form of dramatic poetry.

■ **dramatis personae**

the characters in a work of literature, particularly a drama.

The list of characters printed before the main text of a play or in the program is the dramatis personae.

■ **dream allegory**

see **dream vision.**

■ **dream vision**

a literary convention, chiefly of the Middle Ages. In a dream vision, a story is presented as a literal dream of the narrator. This device was commonly used to teach moral and religious lessons.

Important works of this type are 'The Divine Comedy' by Dante Alighieri, 'Piers Plowman' by William Langland and 'The Pilgrim's Progress' by John Bunyan. Also known as dream allegory.

■ **Dylan Thomas (1914-1953)**

Dylan Thomas was a Welsh poet. He is ranked among the great

20th-century poets. He is also considered as extraordinarily individualistic writer. His Eighteen Poems, published in 1934, created controversy but won him immediate fame. He became more famous with the publication of his other poems like *Twenty-five Poems* (1936), *The Map of Love* (1939), *The World I Breathe* (1939), *Deaths and Entrances* (1946) and *In Country Sleep and Other Poems* (1952). His prose are fragmented into stories and sketches. They are collected in *Portrait of the Artist as a Young Dog* (1940), *Adventures in the Skin Trade* (1955) and *Quite Early One Morning* (1955). In addition, he wrote for the radio *A Child's Christmas in Wales* and *Under Milk Wood*, both of these were published in 1954. Thomas's themes are traditional and over the years, he seemed to pass from religious doubt to joyous faith in God.

■ dysphemism

the substitution of a disagreeable, offensive or disparaging expression to replace an agreeable or inoffensive one.

■ dystopia

an imaginary place in a work of fiction where the characters lead dehumanised, fearful lives.

Jack London's 'The Iron Heel', Yevgeny Zamyatin's 'My', Aldous Huxley's 'Brave New World', George Orwell's 'Nineteen Eighty-four' and Margaret Atwood's 'Handmaid's Tale' portray versions of dystopia.

Aldous Huxley

■ E. M. Forster (879–1970)

Edward Morgan Forster, an English author, was one of the most important British novelists of the 20th century. After his graduation from Cambridge, he started living in Italy and Greece. During World War I, he served with the International Red Cross in Egypt. In 1946, Forster became an honorary fellow of King's College, Cambridge, where he lived until his death. In 1968, he received the Order of Merit.

Forster's fiction is in the English tradition of the novel of manners. In his novels, he explores the emotional and sensual deficiencies of the English middle class. His first novel, *Where Angels Fear to Tread*, appeared in 1905, followed by *The Longest Journey* (1907), *A Room with a View* (1908) and *Howard's End* (1910). His last and most widely acclaimed novel, *A Passage to India* (1924), treats the relations between a group of British colonials and native Indians. His short stories are collected in *The Celestial Omnibus* (1911) and *The Eternal Moment* (1928).

His notable collections of non-fiction essays and literary criticism are *Abinger Harvest* (1936) and *Two Cheers for Democracy* (1951).

■ echo

the repetition of particular sounds, syllables, words or lines in poetry.

■ echo verse

a form of poem in which a word or two at the end of a line appears as an echo constituting the entire following line. The echo, either the same word or syllable or a homophone, often changes the meaning in a flippant, cynical or punning response.

■ eclogue

in classical literature, a poem featuring rural themes and structured as a dialogue among shepherds. Eclogues often took specific poetic forms, such as elegies or love poems. Some were written as the Soliloquy of a shepherd. In later centuries, 'eclogue' came to refer to any poem that was in the pastoral tradition or that had a dialogue or monologue structure.

A classical example of an eclogue is Virgil's 'Eclogues', also known as 'Bucolics'. Giovanni Boccaccio,

Edmund Spenser andrew Marvell, Jonathan Swift and Louis MacNeice also wrote eclogues.

Jonathan Swift

■ edda

either of two collections of mythological, heroic and aphoristic Icelandic poetry from the 12th and 13th centuries.

■ Edgar Allan Poe (1809-1849)

Edgar Allan Poe was an American poet and a critic. He also wrote short stories. He is considered as one of the most brilliant and original writers in America and also the father of the modern detective story. His first book, *Tamerlane and Other Poems*, was published in 1827 and was followed by two more volumes of verse in 1829 and 1831. In 1835, he became the editor of the *Southern Literary Messenger* in Richmond. In 1938, he published *The Narrative of Arthur Gordon Pym* and edited *Burton's Gentleman's Magazine* (1839–40) and *Graham's Magazine* (1841–42). The criticism he made in these magazines made him a respected and feared critic. Some of his magazine stories were collected as *Tales of the Grotesque and Arabesque* (1840). In 1844, he worked on the *Evening Mirror* and later edited and owned the *Broadway Journal.* In 1845, *The Raven and Other Poems* won him fame as a poet, both at home and abroad. In 1846, he wrote *The Literati of New York City* for *Godey's Lady's Book.* Some of his famous poems were *To Helen, The Raven, The City in the Sea, The Bells* and *Annabel Lee.*

■ Edith Newbold Jones Wharton (1862–1937)

Edith Newbold Jones was an American novelist, born in New York City. She was noted for her subtle, ironic and superbly crafted fictional studies of New York society at the turn of the 20th century. She was educated privately in New York and in Europe. She married Edward Wharton in 1885. After a few years of marriage, Edward Wharton became mentally ill and the burden of caring for him fell upon his wife. Finally, in 1913, the couple got divorced.

Edith Newbold Jones' early stories and tales were collected in *The Greater Inclination* (1899), *Crucial Instances* (1901) and *The Descent of Man* (1904).

The novella *Ethan Frome* (1911) was one of her best-known, most successful and least characteristic works. Her many other novels are *The Valley of Decision* (1902), *The Custom of the Country* (1913), *Hudson River Bracketed* (1929) and its sequel, *The Gods Arrive* (1932) and an unfinished work, *The Buccaneers* (1938). Collections of her short stories include *Xingu and Other Stories* (1916), *Certain People* (1930) and *Ghosts* (1937). Wharton is also the author of travel books (like the Italian Backgrounds), literary criticism and poetry. In 1915, she was awarded the Cross of the Legion of Honour by the French government, for her services during World War I.

■ Edmund Spenser (1552-1599)

Edmund Spenser was an English poet. He was not only a master of metre and language but a profound moral poet as well. Spenser first published 12 pastoral eclogues of *The Shepheardes Calender* in 1579. Spenser went to London, where he apparently sought court preferment and publication of the first three books of *The Faerie Queene* in 1589. His poem *Complaints* and elegy *Daphnaida* both appeared in 1591. In 1595, *Colin Clouts Come Home Againe* and *Astrophel* were published. In the same year, *Amoretti*, Spenser's sonnet sequence and *Epithalamion*, a beautiful and complex wedding poem in honour of his marriage in 1594, were also published. Also in 1596, the first six books of *The Faerie Queene*, Spenser's unfinished masterpiece, appeared. The excellence of *The Faerie Queene* lies in the complexity and depth of Spenser's moral vision and in the Spenserian stanza

■ Edmund Waller (1606-1687)

Edmund Waller was an English poet who became a prominent speaker in Parliament at a young age. His early poems are addressed to Sacharissa, Lady Dorothy Sidney. She refused to marry him, though he had been married twice. At first, he was an anti royalist but later on, he supported Charles I against Parliament and conceived *Waller's plot* (1643) to secure the city of London for the king. His plot was discovered and he was banished but was pardoned in 1651. His contribution rests on his style, most notably, the development of the heroic couplet, but his verses were noted for its smoothness and polish. The first collection of his works appeared in 1645 and immediately went through several editions. *Go, Lovely Rose* and *On a Girdle* are his best-known lyrics.

■ Edmund White (1940–)

Edmund White was an American writer. He was born in Cincinnati. He graduated from the University of Michigan (B.A., 1962). White is one of the best known and probably the finest stylist—of the openly gay writers who came to public attention in the 1970s and 80s. His first novel, *Forgetting Elena* (1973), the tale of a young amnesiac's struggle to reassemble his life, was highly stylised and linguistically inventive, as was *Nocturnes* for the King of Naples (1978). His later works concentrate on the struggles, pleasures and political stances of members of contemporary America's male homosexual community.

Some of his other works are the novel *The Married Man* (2000) and short stories, e.g., those in *Skinned Alive* (1995). His non-fiction includes *The Joy of Gay* Sex (co-author, 1977), *States of Desire: Travels in Gay America* (1980), a monumental biography of Jean Genet (1993) and a study of Paris entitled *The Flâneur* (2001).

■ Edwardian

describes cultural conventions identified with the period of the reign of Edward VII of England (1901-1910). Writers of the Edwardian Age typically displayed a strong reaction against the propriety and conservatism of the Victorian Age. Their work often exhibits distrust of authority in religion, politics and art and expresses strong doubts about the soundness of conventional values. Writers of this era include George Bernard Shaw, H. G. Wells and Joseph Conrad.

■ Edwardian age

see **Edwardian.**

■ Edwin Arlington Robinson (1869-1935)

Edwin Arlington Robinson was an American poet. He is best remembered for his short poems. Many critics consider him as the greatest poet in the United States. His first volume of verse, *The Torrent and the Night Before* (1896), was revised and reissued as *The Children of the Night* (1897). The critics poorly received the third volume of verse *Captain Craig* (1902). He achieved critical recognition with *The Man against the Sky* (1916). After that, he concentrated on long psychological narrative poems, such as *Avon's Harvest* (1921). *The Man Who Died Twice* was published in 1924 and he received a Pulitzer Prize for it. Some of his other works include *Dionysus in Doubt* (1925) and the Arthurian romances *Merlin* (1917), *Lancelot* (1920) and *Tristram* (1928). He also won a Pulitzer Prize for *Tristram*. His most lasting work is probably his early verse *Miniver Cheevy* and *Richard Cory*. Volumes of his collected poems were published in 1921 and he got a Pulitzer Prize for it. In 1937, his next volume of poems was published.

■ eidillion or eidyllion

see **idyll.**

■ ekphrasis or ecphrasis

in modern usage, the vivid literary description of a specific work of art, such as a painting, sculpture, tapestry, church and the like. Originally, the term was more broadly applied to a description in words of any experience, person, or thing.

■ Electra complex

a daughter's amorous obsession with her father.

The term Electra complex comes from the plays of Euripides and Sophocles entitled 'Electra', in which the character Electra drives her brother Orestes to kill their mother and her lover in revenge for the murder of their father.

■ elegiac

a dactylic hexameter couplet, with the second line having only an unaccented syllable in the third and sixth feet; also, of or relating to the period in Greece when elegies written in such couplets flourished, about the seventh century B.C.; also, relating to an elegy.

■ elegiac stanza

see **heroic quatrain**.

■ elegy

a lyric poem that laments the death of a person or the eventual death of all people. In a conventional elegy, set in a classical world, the poet and subject are spoken of as shepherds. In modern criticism, the word elegy is often used to refer to a poem that is melancholy or mournfully contemplative.

John Milton's 'Lycidas' and Percy Bysshe Shelley's 'Adonais' are two examples of this form.

■ elision

the omission of a letter or syllable as a means of contraction, generally to achieve a uniform metrical pattern, but sometimes to smooth the pronunciation. Most such omissions are marked with an apostrophe. Specific types of elision include aphaeresis, apocope, syncope, synaeresis and synaloepha.

Elizabethan Age

a period of great economic growth, religious controversy and nationalism, closely associated with the reign of Elizabeth I of England (1558-1603). The Elizabethan Age is considered a part of the general Renaissance — that is, the flowering of arts and literature — that took place in Europe during the fourteenth through sixteenth centuries. The era is considered the golden age of English literature. The most important dramas in English and a great deal of lyric poetry were produced during this period and modern English criticism began around this time.

The notable authors of the period — Philip Sidney, Edmund Spenser, Christopher Marlowe, William Shakespeare, Ben Jonson, Francis Bacon and John Donne — are among the best in all of English literature.

Elizabethan drama

English comic and tragic plays produced during the Renaissance, or more narrowly, those plays written during the last years of and few years after Queen Elizabeth's reign. William Shakespeare is considered an Elizabethan dramatist in the broader sense, although most of his work was produced during the reign of James I.

Examples of Elizabethan comedies include John Lyly's 'The Woman in the Moone', Thomas Dekker's 'The Roaring Girl'and William Shakespeare's 'Twelfth Night'. Examples of Elizabethan tragedies include William Shakespeare's 'Antony and Cleopatra', Thomas Kyd's 'The Spanish Tragedy' and John Webster's 'The Tragedy of the Duchess of Malfi'.

ellipsis

the omission of a word or words necessary to complete a grammatical construction, but which is easily understood by the reader, such as 'the virtues I esteem' for 'the virtues which I esteem'. Also, the marks (. . .) or (—) denoting an omission or pause.

emblem poems

see **pattern poetry.**

empathy

1. a sense of shared experience, including emotional and physical feelings, with someone or something other than oneself. Empathy is often used to describe the response of a reader to a literary character. An example of an empathic passage is William Shakespeare's description in his narrative poem 'Venus and Adonis' of:

the snail, whose tender horns being hit,
Shrinks backward in his shelly cave with pain.

Readers of Gerard Manley Hopkins's 'The Windhover' may experience some of the physical sensations evoked in the description of the movement of the falcon.

2. the feeling or capacity for awareness, understanding and sensitivity one experiences when hearing or reading of some event or activity of another, thus imagining the same sensation as that of those actually experiencing it.

■ Emily Dickinson (1830-1836)

Emily Dickinson was an American poet, is widely as considered as one of the greatest poets in American literature. Her unique, gemlike lyrics are distillations of profound feeling and original intellect, that stand outside the mainstream of 19th-century. Her creative peak seems to have been reached in the period from 1858 to 1862. She published only seven poems during her lifetime. Dickinson wrote love poetry that indicates a strong attachment. The chief tension in her work comes from a different source: her inability to accept the orthodox religious faith of her day and her longing for its spiritual comfort. Her verse are noted for their style and wit and directness of statement and its bold and startling imagery has won enormous acclaim and had a great influence on 20th-century poetry. Dickinson's posthumous fame began when Mabel Loomis Todd and Higginson edited and published her two volumes of poems.

■ Emma Lazarus (1849-1887)

Emma Lazarus was first successful Jewish American author and was celebrated in her day as an important American poet. She was part of the late nineteenth century New York literary elite. Her early poems and translations show that she had a strong classical education and a mastery of German and French. She wrote bold, powerful poetry and essays protesting the rise of anti-Semitism and arguing for Russian immigrants' rights. Enraged by the Russian pogroms of the 1880s, she became an impassioned spokeswoman for Judaism, writing many essays and the book of poems, *Songs of a Semite* (1882), which contains her best work. She wrote verses and sonnets. Her early verse includes *Admetus* and *Other Poems* (1871) and *The Spagnoletto* (1876), a poetic drama. Her sonnet about the Statue of Liberty, *The New Colossus*, was engraved on the statue's pedestal. Her other work includes translations of *Heine.*

■ emphasis

a deliberate stress of articulation on a word or phrase so as to give an impression of particular significance to it by the more marked pronunciation. In writing, emphasis is indicated by the use of italics or underlining.

■ enallage

the effective use of a grammatically incorrect part of speech in place of the correct form, e.g., present tense in place of past tense, plural for singular, etc.

■ enargia

see **ekphrasis.**

■ encomium

a speech or composition in high praise of a person, object or event.

■ end rhyme

a rhyme occurring in the terminating word or syllable of one line of poetry with that of another line, as opposed to internal rhyme.

■ end-stopped

denoting a line of verse in which a logical or rhetorical pause occurs at the end of the line, usually marked with a period, comma, or semicolon.

■ English sonnet

see **sonnet.**

■ enjambment

the running over of the sense and structure of a line of verse or a couplet into the following verse or couplet.

Andrew Marvell's 'To His Coy Mistress' is structured as a series of enjambments, as in lines 11-12: 'My vegetable love should grow/Vaster than empires and more slow'.

■ Enlightenment

an eighteenth-century philosophical movement. It began in France but had a wide impact throughout Europe and America. Thinkers of the Enlightenment valued reason and believed that both the individual and society could achieve a state of perfection. Corresponding to this essentially humanist vision was a resistance to religious authority.

Important figures of the Enlightenment were Denis Diderot and Voltaire in France, Edward Gibbon and David Hume in England and Thomas Paine and Thomas Jefferson in the United States.

■ envelope

a poetic device in which a line, phrase, or stanza is repeated so as to enclose other material.

■ envoi or envoy

a short final stanza of a poem, especially a ballade or sestina, serving as a summary or dedication — like an author's postscript.

■ epanalepsis

a figure of speech in which a word or phrase is repeated after intervening matter.

■ epanaphora

see **anaphora.**

■ epic

a long narrative poem about the adventures of a hero, of great historic or legendary importance. The setting is vast and the action is often given cosmic significance through the intervention of supernatural forces such as gods, angels, or demons. Epics are typically written in a classical style of grand simplicity, with elaborate metaphors and allusions that enhance the symbolic importance of a hero's adventures.

Some well-known epics are Homer's 'Iliad and Odyssey', Virgil's 'Aeneid' and John Milton's 'Paradise Lost'.

epic theatre

a theory of theatrical presentation developed by twentieth-century German playwright Bertolt Brecht. Brecht created a type of drama that the audience could view with complete detachment. He used what he termed 'alienation effects' to create an emotional distance between the audience and the action on stage. Among these effects are: short, self-contained scenes that keep the play from building to a cathartic climax; songs that comment on the action; and techniques of acting that prevent the actor from developing an emotional identity with his role.

Besides the plays of Bertolt Brecht, other plays that utilise epic theatre conventions include those of Georg Buchner, Frank Wedekind, Erwin Piscator and Leopold Jessner.

epigram

a saying that makes the speaker's point quickly and concisely.

Samuel Taylor Coleridge wrote an epigram that neatly sums up the form:

What is an Epigram? A Dwarfish whole,
Its body brevity and wit its soul.

epigraph

a quotation, or a sentence composed for the purpose, placed at the beginning of a literary work or one of its separate divisions, usually suggestive of the theme.

epilogue

a concluding statement or section of a literary work. In dramas, particularly those of the seventeenth and eighteenth centuries, the epilogue is a closing speech, often in verse, delivered by an actor at the end of a play and spoken directly to the audience.

A famous epilogue is Puck's speech at the end of William Shakespeare's 'A Midsummer Night's Dream'.

epinicion or epinician or epinikion

a song in celebration of triumph; an ode in praise of a victory in the Greek games or in war.

epiphany

a sudden revelation of truth, inspired by a seemingly trivial incident.

The term was widely used by James Joyce in his critical writings and the stories in Joyce's 'Dubliners' are commonly called 'epiphanies'.

James Joyce

■ episode

an incident that forms part of a story and is significantly related to it. Episodes may be either self-contained narratives or events that depend on a larger context for their sense and importance.

Examples of episodes include the founding of Wilmington, Delaware in Charles Reade's 'The Disinherited Heir' and the individual events comprising the picaresque novels and medieval romances.

■ episodic plot

see **plot.**

■ epistolary novel

a novel in the form of letters. The form was particularly popular in the eighteenth century.

Samuel Richasrdson's 'Pamela' is considered the first fully developed English epistolary novel.

■ epistrophe

the repetition of a word or expression at the end of successive phrases or verses. Also called epiphora.

■ epitaph

an inscription on a tomb or tombstone, or a verse written on the occasion of a person's death. Epitaphs may be serious or humorous.

Dorothy Parker's epitaph reads, 'I told you I was sick'.

■ epithalamion

a song or poem written to honour and commemorate a marriage ceremony.

Famous examples include Edmund Spenser's 'Epithalamion' and E. E. Cummings's 'Epithalamion'.

■ epithalamium

see **epithalamion.**

■ epithet

a word or phrase, often disparaging or abusive, that expresses a character trait of someone or something.

'The Napoleon of crime' is an epithet applied to Professor Moriarty, archrival of Sherlock Holmes in Arthur Conan Doyle's series of detective stories.

■ epitrite

a metrical foot consisting of three long syllables and one short syllable and denominated first, second, third or fourth, according to the position of the short syllable.

■ epizeuxis

a rhetorical device consisting of the immediate repetition of a word or phrase for emphasis.

■ epode

a type of lyric poem in which a long verse is followed by a shorter one, or the third and last part of an ode; also, the third part of a triadic Greek poem or Pindaric verse following the strophe and the antistrophe.

■ epopee

an epic poem, or the history, action or legend, which is the subject of an epic poem.

epos

an epic poevvm; also a number of poems of an epic theme but which are not formally united.

epyllion

a brief narrative work in classic poetry written in dactylic hexameter. It commonly dealt with mythological themes, often with a romantic interest and was characterised by vivid description, scholarly allusion and an elevated tone.

equivoke or equivoque

an ambiguous word or phrase capable of more than one interpretation, thus susceptible to use for puns.

Ernest Hemingway (1899 – 1961)

This famous author was born on July 21, 1899, in the village of Oak Park, Illinois, close to the prairies and woods west of Chicago.

He began his career by reporting for the *Kansas City Star* where he learned to get to the heart of a story with direct, simple sentences. His first widely successful and acclaimed novel was *A Farewell to Arms.* Ernest learned the literary sparseness and compression in Europe in the 1920s. Hemingway used these methods in short stories and novels that captured the attention of both critics and the public.

In the years following World War II, he published the novella, *The Old Man and the Sea*, which was a major success. This work led to his Pulitzer Prize in 1952. Two years later, he received the Nobel Prize. He died in July 1961 in Ketchum, Idaho. But as he had hoped, his writing lives on.

erziehungsroman

see **bildungsroman.**

essay

a prose composition with a focused subject of discussion. The term was coined by Michel de Montaigne to describe his 1580 collection of brief, informal reflections on himself and on various topics relating to human nature. An essay can also be a long, systematic discourse.

An example of a longer essay is John Locke's 'An Essay Concerning Human Understanding'.

eulogy

a speech or writing in praise of the character or accomplishments of a person.

euphemism

the substitution of an agreeable or inoffensive expression to replace one that might offend or suggest something unpleasant, for example, 'he is at rest' is a euphemism for 'he is dead'.

euphony

harmony or beauty of sound which provides a pleasing effect to the ear, usually sought-for in poetry for effect. It is achieved not only by the selection of individual word-sounds, but also by their relationship in the repetition, proximity and flow of sound patterns.

■ **euphuism**

an ornate Elizabethan style of writing, marked by the excessive use of alliteration, antithesis and mythological similes. The term derives from the elaborate and affected style of John Lyly's 16th century romance, 'Euphues'.

■ **Evelyn Arthur St. John Waugh (1903–66)**

Evelyn Arthur St. John Waugh was an English writer. He was considered the greatest satirist of his generation. Educated at Oxford, he was briefly an art student and a teacher but spent much of his time travelling. He served with distinction in World War II. Waugh burst upon the literary scene with a group of hilarious novels satirising 20th-century life with savage and sophisticated wit, they include *Decline and Fall* (1928), *Vile Bodies* (1930) and *A Handful of Dust* (1934). He was even more mordantly satiric in *Black Mischief* (1932) and *Scoop* (1938), both treating Africa and *Put Out More Flags* (1942), a fictional comment on the English war effort. His most popular novel, *Brideshead Revisited* (1945), recounts the spiritual regeneration of a wealthy Catholic family.

Collectively known as *The Sword of Honour Trilogy*, his three World War II novels, *Men at Arms* (1952), *Officers and Gentlemen* (1955) and *The End of the Battle* (1961), display Waugh's customary ironic wit. He also wrote amusing travel books, biographies of Rossetti (1928) and Edmund Campion (1935) and the autobiographical *A Little Learning* (1964).

■ **exact rhyme**

see **perfect rhyme.**

■ **exempla**

see **exemplum.**

■ **exemplum**

a tale with a moral message. This form of literary sermonising flourished during the Middle Ages, when exempla appeared in collections known as 'example-books'.

The works of Geoffrey Chaucer are full of exempla.

■ **existentialism**

a predominantly twentieth-century philosophy concerned with the nature and perception of human existence. There are two major strains of existentialist thought: atheistic and Christian. Followers of atheistic existentialism believe that the individual is alone in a godless universe and that the basic human condition is one of suffering and loneliness. Nevertheless, because there are no fixed values, individuals can create their own characters — indeed, they can shape themselves — through the exercise of free will. The atheistic strain culminates in and is popularly associated with the works of Jean-Paul Sartre. The Christian existentialists, on the other hand, believe that only in God may people find freedom from life's anguish. The two strains hold certain beliefs in common: that existence cannot be fully understood or described through empirical effort; that anguish is a universal element of life; that individuals must bear responsibility for their actions; and that there is no common standard of behaviour or perception for religious and ethical matters.

Existentialist thought figures prominently in the works of such authors as Eugene Ionesco, Franz Kafka, Fyodor Dostoyevsky, Simone de Beauvoir, Samuel Beckett and Albert Camus.

■ expatriates

see **expatriatism.**

■ expatriatism

the practice of leaving one's country to live for an extended period in another country.

Literary expatriates include English poets Percy Bysshe Shelley and John Keats in Italy, Polish novelist Joseph Conrad in England, American writers Richard Wright, James Baldwin, Gertrude Stein and Ernest Hemingway in France and Trinidadian author Neil Bissondath in Canada.

Richard Wright

■ exposition

writing intended to explain the nature of an idea, thing, or theme. Expository writing is often combined with description, narration, or argument. In dramatic writing, the exposition is the introductory material, which presents the characters, setting and tone of the play.

An example of dramatic exposition occurs in many nineteenth-century drawing-room comedies in which the butler and the maid open the play with relevant talk about their master and mistress; in composition, exposition relays factual information, as in encyclopedia entries.

■ expressionism

an indistinct literary term, originally used to describe an early twentieth-century school of German painting. The term applies to almost any mode of unconventional, highly subjective writing that distorts reality in some way.

Advocates of Expressionism include dramatists George Kaiser, Ernst Toller, Luigi Pirandello, Federico Garcia Lorca, Eugene O'Neill and Elmer Rice; poets George Heym, Ernst Stadler, August Stramm, Gottfried Benn and Georg Trakl; and novelists Franz Kafka and James Joyce.

■ extended metaphor

a metaphor which is drawn-out beyond the usual word or phrase to extend throughout a stanza or an entire poem, usually by using multiple comparisons between the unlike objects or ideas.

■ **extended monologue**

see **monologue.**

■ **fable**

a prose or verse narrative intended to convey a moral. Animals or inanimate objects with human characteristics often serve as characters in fables. A famous fable is Aesop's 'The Tortoise and the Hare'.

■ **fabliau**

a ribald and often cynical tale in verse, especially popular in the Middle Ages.

■ **facetiae**

witty or humorous writings or remarks.

■ **fairy tales**

short narratives featuring mythical beings such as fairies, elves and sprites. These tales originally belonged to the folklore of a particular nation or region, such as those collected in Germany by Jacob and Wilhelm Grimm. Two other celebrated writers of fairy tales are Hans Christian Andersen and Rudyard Kipling.

■ **falling action**

see **denouement.**

■ **fantasy**

a literary form related to mythology and folklore. Fantasy literature is typically set in non-existent realms and features supernatural beings. Notable examples of fantasy literature are 'The Lord of the Rings' by J. R. R. Tolkien and 'the Gormenghast trilogy' by Mervyn Peake.

■ **farce**

a form of humour based on exaggerated, improbable incongruities. Farce involves rapid shifts in action and emotion, as well as slapstick comedy and extravagant dialogue. Malvolio, in Shakespeare's Twelfth Night, is a farcical character.

■ **fatal flaw**

see **hamartia.**

■ **feet**

see **foot.**

■ **feminine ending**

an extra unaccented syllable at the end of an iambic or anapaestic line of poetry, often used in blank verse.

■ **feminine rhyme**

a rhyme occurring on an unaccented final syllable, as in dining and shining or motion and ocean. Feminine rhymes are double or disyllabic rhymes and are common in the heroic couplet.

■ **feminist criticism**

an approach to literature that seeks to correct or supplement what may be regarded as a predominantly male-dominated critical perspective with a feminist consciousness. Feminist criticism places literature in a social context and uses a broad range of disciplines, including history, sociology, psychology and linguistics, to provide a perspective sensitive to feminist issues. Feminist theories also attempt to understand representation from a woman's point of view and to explain women's writing strategies as specific to their social conditions.

■ femme fatale

a French phrase with the literal translation 'fatal woman'. A femme fatale is a sensuous, alluring woman who often leads men into danger or trouble.

A classic example of the femme fatale is the nameless character in Billy Wilder's 'The Seven Year Itch', portrayed by Marilyn Monroe in the film adaptation.

■ fescennine verses

poetry of a personal nature, lacking moral or sexual restraints, commonly extemporised at rustic weddings in Fescennia, Rome and other ancient Italian cities.

■ festschrift

a collection of essays written in honour of a distinguished scholar and presented to him or her to mark some special occasion.

Examples of festschriften are 'Worlds of Jewish Prayer: A Festschrift in Honour of Rabbi Zalman M. Schachter-Shalom'i and 'The Organist as Scholar: Essays in Memory of Russell Saunders'.

■ fiction

any story that is the product of imagination rather than a documentation of fact. Characters and events in such narratives may be based in real life but their ultimate form and configuration is a creation of the author.

Geoffrey Chaucer's 'The Canterbury Tales', Laurence Sterne's 'Tristram Shandy' and Margaret Mitchell's 'Gone with the Wind' are examples of fiction.

■ fictional

relating to literature in which there are internal characters, apart from the author and his audience; opposed to thematic.

■ figurative language

a technique in writing in which the author temporarily interrupts the order, construction, or meaning of the writing for a particular effect. This interruption takes the form of one or more figures of speech such as hyperbole, irony, or simile. Figurative language is the opposite of literal language, in which every word is truthful, accurate and free of exaggeration or embellishment.

■ figure of speech

a mode of expression in which words are used out of their literal meaning or out of their ordinary use in order to add beauty or emotional intensity or to transfer the poet's sense impressions by comparing or identifying one thing with another that has a meaning familiar to the reader. Some important figures of speech are: simile, metaphor, personification, hyperbole and symbol.

fin de siecle

a French term meaning 'end of the century'. The term is used to denote the last decade of the nineteenth century, a transition period when writers and other artists abandoned old conventions and looked for new techniques and objectives.

Two writers commonly associated with the fin de siecle mindset are Oscar Wilde and George Bernard Shaw.

Firdausi (940-1020)

Abul Kasim Mansur commonly known as Firdausi. He was a Persian poet and wrote the famous Persian epic *Shah Namah* [the book of kings]. He received a thorough education in Muslim learning and in the Persian language and antiquities. The course of his life is not certain. He was poet at the court of Mahmud of Ghazna. He undertook epic history of Persia and glorified the Persia's past. His work was dedicated to the king but the king did not pay him well because of this he wrote a savage satire on the king and fled. After that, he kept on going from court to court and finally arrived at his homeland during his old age. His poem, in 60,000 verses, is the first great work of modern Persian literature. Firdausi set the mark for Persian poetry with his even rhyme, stately cadences and continuous flow. Illiterate tribes people recite the long sections of the poem. One of the masterpieces of world art is the Houghton *Shah-Nameh* illustrated version of *Shah Namah*.

first person

see **point of view.**

fit or fytte

an archaic term for the division of a poem, i.e., a stanza or canto.

fixed form

a poem that may be categorised by the pattern of its lines, meter, rhythm, or stanzas. A sonnet is a fixed form of poetry because by definition it must have fourteen lines. Other fixed forms include limerick, sestina and villanelle. However, poems written in a fixed form may not always fit into categories precisely, because writers sometimes vary traditional forms to create innovative effects.

flashback

a device used in literature to present action that occurred before the beginning of the story. Flashbacks are often introduced as the dreams or recollections of one or more characters.

Flashback techniques are often used in films, where they are typically set off by a gradual changing of one picture to another.

focalisation

in narrative fiction, focalisation answers the questions who sees? and who speaks?

focaliser

a term for the holder of the point of view, whose eyes readers see through.

foil

a character in a work of literature whose physical or psychological qualities contrast strongly with and therefore highlight, the corresponding qualities of another character.

In his Sherlock Holmes stories, Arthur Conan Doyle portrayed Dr. Watson as a man of normal habits and intelligence, making him a foil for the eccentric and wonderfully perceptive Sherlock Holmes.

folk ballad

see **ballad.**

folklore

traditions and myths preserved in a culture or group of people. Typically, these are passed on by word of mouth in various forms—such as legends, songs and proverbs—or preserved in customs and ceremonies. This term was first used by W. J. Thomas in 1846. Sir James Frazer's The Golden Bough is the record of English folklore; myths about the frontier and the Old South exemplify American folklore.

folktale

a story originating in oral tradition. Folktales fall into a variety of categories, including legends, ghost stories, fairy tales, fables and anecdotes based on historical figures and events. Examples of folktales include Giambattista Basile's 'The Pentamerone', which contains the tales of 'Puss in Boots', 'Rapunzel', 'Cinderella' and 'Beauty and the Beast' and Joel Chandler Harris's 'Uncle Remus stories', which represent, transplanted African folktales and American tales about the characters Mike Fink, Johnny Appleseed, Paul Bunyan and Pecos Bill.

foot

the smallest unit of rhythm in a line of poetry. In English-language poetry, a foot is typically one accented syllable combined with one or two unaccented syllables.

There are many different types of feet. When the accent is on the second syllable of a two syllable word (con-tort), the foot is an 'iamb'; the reverse accentual pattern (tor-ture) is a 'trochee'. Other feet that commonly occur in poetry in English are 'anapest', two unaccented syllables followed by an accented syllable as in in-ter-cept and 'dactyl', an accented syllable followed by two unaccented syllables as in su-i-cide.

foreshadowing

a device used in literature to create expectation or to set up an explanation of later developments.

In Charles Dickens's 'Great Expectations', the graveyard encounter at the beginning of the novel, between Pip and the escaped convict Magwitch, foreshadows the baleful atmosphere and events that comprise much of the narrative.

form

the pattern or construction of a work, which identifies its genre and distinguishes it from other genres. Examples of forms include the different genres, such as the lyric form or the short story form and various patterns for poetry, such as the verse form or the stanza form.

formalism

in literary criticism, the belief that literature should follow prescribed rules of construction, such as those that govern the sonnet form. Examples of formalism are found in the work of the New Critics and structuralists.

formalist criticism

an approach to literature that focuses on the formal elements of a work, such as its language, structure and tone. Formalist critics offer intense examinations of the relationship between form and meaning in a work, emphasising the subtle complexity sin how a work is arranged. Formalists pay special attention to diction, irony, paradox, metaphor and symbol, as well as larger elements such as plot, characterisation and narrative technique. Formalist critics read literature as an independent work of art rather than as a reflection of the author's state of mind or as a representation of a moment in history. Therefore, anything outside of the work, including historical influences and authorial intent, is generally not examined by formalist critics.

formula literature

often characterised as 'escape literature', formula literature follows a pattern of conventional reader expectations. Romance novels, westerns, science fiction and detective stories are all examples of formula literature; while the details of individual stories vary, the basic ingredients of each kind of story are the same. Formula literature offers happy endings (the hero 'gets the girl', the detective cracks the case), entertains wide audiences and sells tremendously well.

found poem

a poem created from prose found in a non-poetic context, such as advertising copy, brochures, newspapers, product labels, etc. The lines are arbitrarily rearranged into a form patterned on the rhythm and appearance of poetry.

fourteener

an iambic line of fourteen syllables, or seven feet, widely used in English poetry in the middle of the 16th century.

fourteener meter

see **meter.**

Franz Kafka (1883–1924)

Franz Kafka was a German language novelist who was born in Prague. Along with Joyce, Kafka is perhaps the most influential of 20th-century writers. From a middle-class Jewish family from Bohemia, he spent most of his life in Prague. He studied law and then obtained a position in the workmen's compensation division of Austro-Hungarian government. Most of his works were published posthumously. His major novels include *Der Prozess* (1925), *Das Schloss* (1926) and *Amerika* (1927). His proses were remarkable in clarity and precision. Kafka presents a world that is at once real and dreamlike and in which individuals, burdened with guilt, isolation and anxiety, make a futile search for personal salvation. Important stories appearing during his lifetime were *Das Urteil* (1913), *Die Verwandlung* (1915), *Ein Landarzt* (1919), *In der Strafkolonie* (1920) and *Ein Hungerkünstler* (1922).

■ free verse

poetry that lacks regular metrical and rhyme patterns but that tries to capture the Cadences of everyday speech. The form allows a poet to exploit a variety of rhythmical effects within a single poem.

Free-verse techniques have been widely used in the twentieth century by such writers as Ezra Pound, T. S. Eliot, Carl Sandburg and William Carlos Williams.

Also known as Vers libre.

■ futurism

a flamboyant literary and artistic movement that developed in France, Italy and Russia from 1908 through the 1920s. Futurist theatre and poetry abandoned traditional literary forms. In their place, followers of the movement attempted to achieve total freedom of expression through bizarre imagery and deformed or newly invented words. The Futurists were self-consciously modern artists who attempted to incorporate the appearances and sounds of modern life into their work.

Futurist writers include Filippo Tommaso Marinetti, Wyndham Lewis, Guillaume Apollinaire, Velimir Khlebnikov and Vladimir Mayakovsky.

■ Gabriel García Márquez (1928–)

García Márquez is a Colombian novelist, short-story writer and journalist. Widely considered the greatest living Latin American master of narrative, García Márquez won the Nobel Prize for Literature in 1982. Reflecting the influence of writers such as Jorges Luis Borges, Miguel Angel Asturias and Alejo Carpentier, his work focuses on the physical and moral travail of coastal Colombia, but is given universal meaning in his books. His two masterpieces *One Hundred Years of Solitude* (1967, tr. 1970), his best-known work and *Love in the Time of Cholera* (1985, tr. 1988), present his central themes of violence, solitude and the overwhelming human need for love. García Márquez's style marks a high point in Latin American magic realism. It is rich and lucid, mixing reality and fantasy. Among his other works are *Leaf Storm and Other Stories* (1955, tr. 1972), *No One Writes to the Colonel and Other Stories* (1958, tr. 1968), *Innocent Erendira and Other Stories* (1972, tr. 1978), *The Autumn of the Patriarch* (1975, tr. 1976), *The General in His Labyrinth* (1989, tr. 1990) and *Of Love and Other Demons* (1994, tr. 1995). His non-fiction works are *News of a Kidnapping* (1996, tr. 1997), chronicles related to drug abductions in Colombia.

■ Gabriela Mistral (1889-1957)

Gabriela Mistral was a Chilean poet whose original name was Lucila Godoy Alcayaga. She worked in rural schools in Chile as a teacher and a director and later attained wider acclaim as an educator. Under José Vasconcelos, she revised the Mexican school system. She represented Chile at the League of Nations and the United Nations and she also served as Chilean consul in various European and Latin American cities.

The recurrent themes in her fluent and lyric verse are the mystery of childbearing, the sorrow of a tragic love and a burning desire for justice. She was highly praised for her work in *Sonetos de la muerte*, which was published in 1915. Three major volumes written by her are *Desolación* (1922), *Tala* (1938) and *Lagar* (1954). In 1957, her *Selected Poems* was published. Langston Hughes translated it. She was the first Latin American to be honoured with the Nobel Prize in Literature in 1945.

■ galliambus

in classic poetry, a lyric meter consisting of four iambic dipodies, the last of which is catalectic, dropping the final accent, or a line of four lesser Ionic feet catalectic, varied by anaclasis.

■ gay and lesbian criticism

an approach to literature that focuses on how homosexuals are represented in literature, how they read literature and whether sexuality, as well as gender, is culturally constructed or innate.

■ gender criticism

an approach to literature that explores how ideas about men and women—what is masculine and feminine—can be regarded as socially constructed by particular cultures. Gender criticism expands categories and definitions of what is masculine or feminine and tends to regard sexuality as more complex than merely masculine or feminine, heterosexual or homosexual. See also **feminist criticism, gay and lesbian criticism.**

■ genre

a French word meaning kind or type. The major genres in literature are poetry, fiction, drama and essays. Genre can also refer to more specific types of literature such as comedy, tragedy, epic poetry, or science fiction.

■ genteel tradition

a term coined by critic George Santayana to describe the literary practice of certain late nineteenth-century American writers, especially New Englanders. Followers of the Genteel Tradition emphasised conventionality in social, religious, moral and literary standards.

Some of the best-known writers of the Genteel Tradition are R. H. Stoddard and Bayard Taylor.

George Santayana

■ Geoffrey Chaucer (1340-1400)

Geoffrey Chaucer, an English poet was one of the most important figures in English literature. Chaucer's literary career is divided into three periods. The first period includes his early work (to 1370), which is based on French models, especially the *Roman de la Rose* and the poems of *Guillaume de Machaut*. Chaucer's chief works during this time are the *Book of the Duchess*, an allegorical lament. Chaucer's second period (upto 1387) is known as his Italian period. Major works of this period include *The House of Fame*, *The Parliament of Fowls* and a prose translation of *Boethius' De consolatione philosophiae*. He also wrote a poem, *Legend of Good Women,* which he could not finish. Chaucer's third period showed his full artistic power. He wrote his masterpiece, *The Canterbury Tales*. This unfinished poem is one of the most brilliant works in all literature. Chaucer was a master storyteller and craftsman, but because of a change in the language after 1400, his metrical technique was not fully appreciated until the 18th century.

■ George Bernard Shaw (1856–1950)

Shaw was a prominent Irish playwright and critic. He revolutionised the Victorian stage, which was then dominated by artificial melodramas, by presenting vigorous dramas of ideas. The lengthy prefaces of his plays reveal his command over English prose. He was awarded the Nobel Prize in Literature in 1925.

Shaw left school at 14 to work in an estate agent's office. In 1876, he went to London and for nine years was largely supported by his parents. He wrote five novels, several of them published in small socialist magazines. Shaw was himself a fervent socialist, a member of the Fabian Society and a popular public speaker on behalf of socialism. Work as a journalist led to his becoming a music critic for the Star in 1888 and for the

World in 1890. In 1891, he wrote *The Quintessence of Ibsenism.*

His early plays were published as Plays Pleasant and Unpleasant. The unpleasant plays were *Widower's Houses, On slum landlordism, The Philanderer and Mrs. Warren's Profession.* The pleasant plays were *Arms and the Man*, satirically aiming at romantic attitudes towards love and war, *Candida and You Never Can Tell.* The play *Pygmalion* (1913) was his most successful work.

■ George Eliot (1819–80)

George Eliot, pseudonym for Mary Ann or Marian Evans, was an English novelist. She was born in Arbury, Warwickshire. One of the great English novelists, she was reared in a strict atmosphere of evangelical Protestantism but eventually rebelled and renounced organised religion totally. After her father's death, she became the sub editor (1851) of the Westminster Review and contributed articles. In 1854, she began a long and happy union with G. H. Lewes, which she regarded as marriage, though it involved social ostracism and could have no legal sanction because Lewes's estranged wife was living.

In 1856, Mary Ann began *Scenes of Clerical Life*, a series of realistic sketches first appearing in Blackwood's Magazine under the pseudonym Lewes chose for her, George Eliot. Although not a popular success, the work was well received by literary critics, particularly Dickens and Thackeray. Three novels of provincial life followed—*Adam Bede* (1859), *The Mill on the Floss* (1860) and *Silas Marner* (1861). Although her novels are highly serious, they are marked by compassion and a subtle humour.

■ George Gordon Noel Byron Byron, 6th Baron (1788-1824)

George Gordon Noel Byron Byron, 6th Baron was an English poet and satirist.

Fugitive Pieces (1806) his first volume appeared in 1807 as *Poems on Various Occasions.* This was followed by *Hours of Idleness* (1807). This book received severe criticism from the Edinburgh Review. Byron replied with *English Bards* and *Scotch Reviewers* (1809). He used technique of satire in heroic couplets. This brought him immediate fame. *Cantos I and II of Childe Harold* was published in 1812, after he had returned from his grand tour. *The Giaour* (1813), *The Bride of Abydos* (1813), *The Corsair* (1814), *Lara* (1814), *The Siege of Corinth* (1816) and *Parisina* (1816) followed it. In 1816, Byron was considered a social outcast and he left England. He stayed with Shelley in Switzerland, writing *Canto III of Childe Harold* (1816) and *The Prisoner of Chillon* (1816). He produced *Canto IV of Childe Harold* (1818), *Beppo* (1818) and *Mazeppa* (1819) and began *Don Juan.* Byron was induced to interest himself in the cause of Greek independence. He worked unsparingly with Prince Alexander Mavrocordatos to unify the divergent Greek forces, but caught a fever and died the same year.

■ George Herbert (1593-1633)

George Herbert did his graduation from Cambridge. He was one of the English metaphysical poets. He was the brother of Baron Herbert of Cherbury. He was appointed as a public orator in 1619, so his early determination to enter the church was temporarily deflected. He held the post of orator until 1627. In 1630, he was ordained an Anglican priest and made rector at Bemerton. Because of this, his devotional poems combine a homely familiarity with religious experience and a reverent sense of its magnificence. Quietness of tone, precision of language, metrical versatility and the use of conceits marked his verses. Herbet left all his unpublished poems to his friend Nicholas Ferrar, who had them published as *The Temple* (1633). Herbert also wrote Latin poems and a prose manual of clerical life, *A Priest of the Temple* (first printed in Herbert's Remains, 1652). In the 20th century, the revival of interest in the metaphysical poets has stressed Herbert.

■ Georgian Age

see **Georgian Poets.**

■ Georgian Period

see **Georgian Poets.**

■ Georgian Poets

a loose grouping of English poets during the years 1912-1922. The Georgians reacted against certain literary schools and practices, especially Victorian wordiness, turn-of-the-century aestheticism and contemporary urban realism. In their place, the Georgians embraced the nineteenth-century poetic practices of William Wordsworth and the other Lake Poets. Rupert Brooke, Walter de la Mare and D. H. Lawrence are three of the most prominent poets of the Georgian Period.

■ georgic

a poem about farming and the farmer's way of life, named from Virgil's Georgics. Several English poets in the eighteenth century produced georgics in imitation of Virgil, including John Dyer's 'The Fleece' and James Grainger's 'The Sugar-Cane'.

■ ghazal

a monorhymed Middle Eastern lyric poem in which the first two lines rhyme with a corresponding rhyme in the second line of each succeeding couplet, thus a rhyme scheme of aa, ba, ca, etc.

■ Gilded Age

a period in American history during the 1870s, characterised by political corruption and materialism. A number of important novels of social and political criticism were written during this time. Examples of Gilded Age literature include Henry Adams's 'Democracy' and F. Marion Crawford's 'An American Politician'.

■ gleeman

an old English minstrel. Gleemen sometimes composed their own verses, but often recited poetry written by a scop.

■ gnome

an aphorism, a short statement of proverbial truth. Composers of such verse are known as gnomic poets.

■ goliardic poetry

satiric verse which flourished in the 12th and 13th centuries, usually consisting of a stanza of four 13-syllable lines in feminine rhyme, sometimes with a concluding hexameter. The satire was characteristically a defiance of authority, most particularly directed against the Church.

■ gongorism

named for the 17th century Spanish poet, Luis de Gongora y Argote, a literary style characterised by stilted obscurity and the use of affected devices of embellishment.

■ Gothic

see **Gothicism.**

■ Gothic novel

see **Gothicism.**

■ Gothicism

in literary criticism, works characterised by a taste for the medieval or morbidly attractive. A gothic novel prominently features elements of horror, the supernatural, gloom and violence clanking chains, terror, charnel houses, ghosts, medieval castles and mysteriously slamming doors. The term 'gothic novel' is also applied to novels that lack elements of the traditional Gothic setting but that create a similar atmosphere of terror or dread. Mary Shelley's 'Frankenstein' is perhaps the best-known English work of this kind.

Mary Shelly

■ Graham Greene (1904–91)

Henry Graham Greene was an English novelist and playwright. He was a Roman Catholic convert, who was intensely concerned with the moral problems of humans in relation to God. Some of his novels have been ranked as thrillers and Greene himself called such works as *Stamboul Train* and *The Ministry of Fear* (1943) entertainments to distinguish them from his more serious efforts. His major works, which include *Brighton Rock* (1938), *The Power and the Glory* (1940), *The Heart of the Matter* (1948) and *The End of the Affair* (1951), mark him as a novelist of high distinction. Greene was a superb journalist and many of his novels are set in sites of topical journalistic interest, like *The Quiet American* (1955), *Our Man in Havana* (1958), *A Burnt-Out Case* (1961) and *The Captain and the Enemy* (1980), in Panama. His fine sense of comedy is displayed in the short-story collection *May We Borrow Your Husband?* (1967) and the novel *Travels with My Aunt* (1969). Greene also wrote several plays, including *The Living Room* (1953) and *The Potting Shed* (1957). He is also noted for his short stories, essays, film criticism and film scripts, including the mystery melodrama *The Third Man* (1950).

■ grave

in poetry, a mark (`) indicating that the *e* in the English ending *ed* is to be pronounced for the sake of meter.

■ graveyard school

a group of eighteenth-century English poets who wrote long, picturesque meditations on death. Their works were designed to cause the reader to ponder immortality. The most famous work of this school is Thomas Gray's Elegy Written in a Country Churchyard.

■ great chain of being

the belief that all things and creatures in nature are organised in a hierarchy, from inanimate objects at the bottom to God at the top. This system of belief was popular in the seventeenth and eighteenth centuries. A summary of the concept of the great chain of being can be found in the first epistle of Alexander Pope's 'An essay on Man' and more recently in Arthur O. Lovejoy's 'The Great Chain of Being- A Study of the History of an Idea'.

Arthur O. Lovejoy

grotesque

in literary criticism, the subject matter of a work or a style of expression, characterised by exaggeration, deformity, freakishness and disorder. The grotesque often includes an element of comic absurdity. Early examples of literary grotesque include Francois Rabelais's 'Pantagruel' and Gargantua and Thomas Nashe's 'The Unfortunate Traveller', while more recent examples can be found in the works of Edgar Allan Poe, Evelyn Waugh, Eudora Welty, Flannery O'Connor, Eugene Ionesco, Gunter Grass, Thomas Mann, Mervyn Peake and Joseph Heller, among many others.

Edgar Allan Poe

Günter Grass (1927–)

Günter Grass was a German novelist, lyricist, artist and playwright. He was born in Danzig (now Gdansk, Poland). Writing from his experience in the Luftwaffe and as a prisoner of war, Grass deplores fascist militarism. The anguish of war and the social and political problems that West Germany faced before reunification are the principal concerns of his fiction. His novel *Die Blechtrommel* (1959) brought him world renown. His second novel, *Hundejahre* (1963), is a monumental work that also aroused considerable controversy. His later works mainly reflect a period of intense political activism.

Grass's major 1990s work, the novel *Ein Weites Feld* (1995), was widely criticised for rambling plot-less. His other works include a collection of speeches and open letters entitled *Speak Out!* and the novels *Mariazuehren* (1973) and *Unkenrufe* (1992). In 1999, Grass was awarded the Nobel Prize in Literature for his frolicsome black fables (that) portray the forgotten face of history.

haiku

a Japanese form of poetry, also known as hokku. It consists of three unrhymed lines of five, seven and five syllables. The elusive flavour of the form, however, lies more in its touch and tone than in its syllabic structure. Deeply embedded in Japanese culture and strongly influenced by Zen Buddhism, haiku are very brief descriptions of nature that convey some implicit insight or essence of a moment. Traditionally, they contain either a direct or oblique reference to a season.

half rhyme

a near rhyme; also, an apocopated rhyme in which the rhyme occurs only on the first syllable of the rhyming word, as in blue and truly or sum and trumpet.

hamartia

in tragedy, the event or act that leads to the hero's or heroine's downfall. This term is often incorrectly used as a synonym for tragic flaw. In Richard Wright's 'Native Son', the act that seals Bigger Thomas's fate is his first impulsive murder.

Harivanshrai Bachchan (1907-2003)

Harivanshrai Bachchan, an Indian poet is considered as the great romantic voice of Hindi poetry, who penned rebellious lines of rejection of tradition. He enriched Hindi through his translations of major writings. Besides *Rubaiyat*, he will also be remembered for his Hindi translations of Shakespeare's *Mac Beth* and *Othello* and also *The Bhagvad Gita*. His stardom was unique in Hindi literature. It was mostly the gift of *Madhushaala*. It is undoubtedly one of the most enduring works of modern Hindi literature. It has been translated into English and regional Indian languages such as Bengali, Marathi and Malayalam. The only thing of real significance to come from Bachchan's pen at a later stage was his autobiography in four volumes, now considered one of the landmarks in the evolution of the genre in the Hindi language. Bachchan was nominated to the Rajya Sabha in 1966 and received the Sahitya Akademi award three years later. In 1976, he was honoured with the Padma Bhushan for his immense contribution to Hindi literature. He was also honoured with the Saraswati Samman, the Soviet land Nehru Award and the Lotus Award of the Afro-Asian writer's conference, for his unique contribution to the world of letters.

Harlem Renaissance

the Harlem Renaissance of the 1920s is generally considered the first significant movement of black writers and artists in the United States. During this period, new and established black writers published more fiction and poetry than ever before, the first influential black literary journals were established and black authors and artists received their first widespread recognition and serious critical appraisal. Among the major writers associated with this period are Claude McKay, Jean Toomer, Countee Cullen, Langston

Hughes, Arna Bontemps, Nella Larsen and Zora Neale Hurston.

Langston Hughes

Works representative of the Harlem Renaissance include Arna Bontemps's poems 'The Return' and 'Golgotha Is a Mountain', Claude McKay's novel 'Home to Harlem', Nella Larsen's novel 'Passing', Langston Hughes's poem 'The Negro Speaks of Rivers', and the journals 'Crisis' and 'Opportunity', both founded during this period.

Also known as Negro Renaissance and New Negro Movement.

■ Harlequin

a stock character of the commedia dell'arte who occasionally interrupted the action with silly antics. Harlequin first appeared on the English stage in John Day's 'The Travailes of the Three English Brothers'. The San Francisco Mime Troupe is one of the few modern groups to adapt Harlequin to the needs of contemporary satire.

■ head rhyme

see **alliteration.**

■ helicon

a part of the Parnassus, a mountain range in Greece, which was the home of the Muses. The name is used as an allusion to poetic inspiration.

■ Hellenism

imitation of ancient Greek thought or styles. Also, an approach to life that focuses on the growth and development of the intellect. 'Hellenism' is sometimes used to refer to the belief that reason can be applied to examine all human experience. A cogent discussion of Hellenism can be found in Matthew Arnold's 'Culture and Anarchy'.

Matthew Arnold

■ hemistich

the approximate half of a line of poetic verse, usually divided by a caesura. In dramatic poetry, it is used whenever characters exchange short bursts of dialogue rapidly, heightening the effect of quarrelsome disagreement; in classical poetry, such a series is called hemistichomythia. Other types of poetry may use an occasional hemistich to give the effect of emotionally disturbed thought or action.

■ hendecasyllable

a metrical line of eleven syllables.

■ hendiadys

the use of a pair of nouns joined by 'and' where one has the effect of a modifier.

■ Henrik Ibsen (1828–1906)

Ibsen was a renowned Norwegian dramatist and poet. His early years were lonely and miserable. Distressed by the consequences of his family's financial ruin and on his own at sixteen, he first was apprenticed to an apothecary. Not long after this, he began writing poetry and in 1850, he published his first play, *Catilina*, a tragedy in verse. In 1851, he began an extended apprenticeship in the theatre, first as stage manager and playwright with the National Stage in Bergen and in 1857, as theatre director for the Norwegian Theatre in Oslo.

He wrote the bulk of his drama in Italy and in Germany. His career can be divided into three periods. The first phase, that of poetic dramas, dealt primarily with historical themes, folklore and romantic pageantry. He became famous with the publication of *Love's Comedy* (1862). In 1866, he reached prominent stature as a dramatist, when he published the first of his major works, *Brand*, the tragedy of an idealist. No playwright has exerted greater influence on 20th-century drama. His plays are continually revived in the United States and Europe.

■ Henry James (1843–1916)

Henry James was an American novelist and critic born in New York City. A master of the psychological novel, James was an innovator in technique and one of the most distinctive prose stylists in English.

Educated privately by tutors in Europe and the United States, he entered Harvard law school in 1862. James wrote critical articles and reviews for the Atlantic Monthly, a periodical in which several of his novels later appeared in serial form.

James devoted himself to literature and travel. In his early novels, including *Roderick Hudson* (1876), *The American* (1877), *Daisy Miller* (1879) and *The Portrait of a Lady* (1881), as well as some of his later work, James contrasts the sophisticated, though somewhat staid, Europeans with the innocent, eager, though often brash, Americans. In his last and perhaps his greatest novels, *The Wings of the Dove* (1902), *The Ambassadors* (1903) and *The Golden Bowl* (1904), all with an international theme, James reached his highest development in the portrayal of the intricate subtleties of character and in the use of a complex, convoluted style to express delicate nuances of thought.

heptameter

a line of verse consisting of seven metrical feet. It is also called a septenarius, especially in Latin prosody.

Herbert George Wells (1866–1946)

Wells, besides being famous for his works of science fiction and an imaginative social thinker, working assiduously to remove all vestiges of Victorian social, was a renowned English author. He was apprenticed to a draper at 14 and later was able to attend the University of London through grants and scholarships (graduated in 1888). Inspired by the teaching of T. H. Huxley, Wells taught biology until 1893, when he began his career as a novelist. His early books were full of fantasy and fascinating pseudoscien-tific speculations, which exemplify the political and social beliefs of his time. They include *The Time Machine* (1895), *The Wonderful Visit* (1895), *The Invisible Man* (1897) and *The War of the Worlds* (1898). In the novels of his middle period, he turned from the fantastic to the realistic. These books, considered his finest achievement, include *Kipps* (1905), *Tono-Bungay* (1909) and *The History of Mr. Polly* (1910). Included among his final works, which became increasingly pessimistic, are *The World of William Clissold* (1926), *The Shape of Things to Come* (1933), *World Brain* (1938) and *Mind at the End of Its Tether* (1945).

hero/heroine

the principal sympathetic character (male or female) in a literary work. Heroes and heroines typically exhibit admirable traits idealism, courage and integrity, for example. Famous heroes and heroines include Pip in Charles Dickens's 'Great Expectations', the anonymous narrator in Ralph Ellison's 'Invisible Man' and Sethe in Toni Morrison's 'Beloved'.

heroic couplet

two successive lines of rhymed poetry in iambic pentameter, so called for its use in the composition of epic poetry in the 17th and 18th centuries. In neo-classical usage, the two lines were required to express a complete thought, thus a closed couplet, with a subordinate pause at the end of the first line. Heroic couplets, which are well suited to antithesis and parallelism, are also often used for epigrams.

heroic line

the meter and length of a line of verse in epic or heroic poetry. This varies by language and time period. For example, in English poetry, the heroic line is iambic pentameter (a verse with five iambic feet); in French, the alexandrine (a verse with six iambic feet); in classical literature, dactylic hexameter (a verse with six dactylic feet).

■ heroic quatrain or heroic verse

so named because it is the form in which epic poetry of heroic exploits is generally written, its rhyme scheme is abab, composed in ten-syllable iambic verse in English, hexameter in Greek and Latin, ottava rima in Italian.

■ heroine

see **hero/heroine.**

■ heterometric composition

a poem written in meter but with lines of differing length, e.g. one line of tetrameter, one of pentameter, one of dimeter etc.

■ heteronym

see **homonym.**

■ hexameter

a line of verse consisting of six metrical feet. The term, however, is usually used for dactylic hexameter, consisting of dactyls and spondees, the meter in which the Greek and Latin epics were written.

■ hiatus

see **elision.**

■ higgledy-piggledy

see **double dactyl.**

■ historical criticism

the study of a work, based on its impact on the world of the time period in which it was written. Examples of post-modern historical criticism can be found in the work of Michel Foucault, Hayden White, Stephen Greenblatt and Jonathan Goldberg.

■ hokku

see **haiku.**

■ Holocaust literature

literature influenced by or written about the Holocaust of World War II. Such literature includes true stories of survival in concentration camps, escape and life after the war, as well as fictional works and poetry. Representative works of Holocaust literature include Saul Bellow's 'Mr. Sammler's Planet', Anne Frank's 'The Diary of a Young Girl', Jerzy Kosinski's 'The Painted Bird', Arthur Miller's 'Incident at Vichy', Czeslaw Milosz's 'Collected Poems', William Styron's 'Sophie's Choice' and Art Spiegelman's 'Maus'.

■ Homer (Around 700 B.C.)

Homer is regarded as the first European poet and was a principal figure of ancient Greek. Legends about him were numerous in ancient times. It is believed that he was blind. It is considered that *The Iliad* and *The Odyssey* are the works of two different people. The Homeric question was the great dispute of scholarship in the 19th century. Recent evidence strongly suggests *The Iliad* and *The Odyssey* are each the product of one poet's work, developed out of older legendary matter. Two epic poems are attributed to Homer, *The Iliad* and *The Odyssey.* Ranked among the great works of Western literature, these two poems together constitute the prototype for all subsequent Western epic poetry. They are composed in a literary type of Greek. The atmosphere of adventure and fate in *The Odyssey,* contrasts with the heavier tone and tragic grandeur of *The Iliad.*

■ homeric simile

an elaborate, detailed comparison, written as a simile and many lines in length. An example of an epic simile from John Milton's Paradise Lost follows:

Angel Forms, who lay entranced
Thick as autumnal leaves that strow the brooks
In Vallombrosa, where the Etrurian shades
High over-arched embower; or scattered sedge
Afloat, when with fierce winds Orion armed
Hath vexed the Red-Sea coast, whose waves o'erthrew
Busiris and his Memphian chivalry
While with perfidious hatred they pursued
The sojourners of Goshen, who beheld
From the safe shore their floating carcasses
And broken chariot-wheels.

Also known as Epic Simile.

■ homonym

one of two or more words which are identical in pronunciation and spelling, but different in meaning, as the noun 'bear' and the verb 'bear'.

■ Horace (65 B.C.-8 B.C.)

Quintus Horatius Flaccus is the original name of Horace. He was one of the greatest lyric Latin poets. His *first book of Satires* appeared in 35 B.C., the *second book of Satires* in 29 B.C., *Three books of Odes* in 24 B.C. and *The first book of Epistles* in 20 B.C. The *fourth book of Odes, the second book of Epistles, a hymn* (the Carmen Saeculare) and *the Ars Poetica* or *Epistle to the Pisos,* appeared in 13 B.C. Horace was an unrivalled lyric poet. As his genius matured, his themes turned from personal vilification to more generalised satire and to literary criticism. He gives a vivid picture of contemporary Roman society and represents especially the spirit of the Augustan age of Rome—a time of peace, when the arts were cultivated earnestly without pretense. His early poems show the influence of the Greek Archilochus, but his later verse displays complete and individualised adaptation of Greek metres to Latin. He had much influence on European poetry.

■ horatian ode

an ode relating to or resembling the works or style of the Roman poet, Horace, consisting of a series of uniform stanzas, complex in their metrical system and rhyme scheme. The Greek form is called an Aeolic ode. Horatian odes are characteristically less elaborate and more restrained than Pindaric odes.

■ horatian satire

see **satire.**

hovering accent

in scansion, a stress which is thought of as being equally distributed over two adjacent syllables, a concept proposed to cover an accent not in alignment with the expected metrical ictus.

hudibrastic verse

a mock-heroic humorous poem written in octosyllabic couplets, after Hudibras, a satirical poem by Samuel Butler.

humanism

a philosophy that places faith in the dignity of humankind and rejects the medieval perception of the individual as a weak, fallen creature. 'Humanists' typically believe in the perfectibility of human nature and view reason and education as the means to that end.

Humanist thought is represented in the works of Marsilio Ficino, Ludovico Castelvetro, Edmund Spenser, John Milton, Dean John Colet, Desiderius Erasmus, John Dryden, Alexander Pope, Matthew Arnold and Irving Babbitt.

Edmund Spenser

humours

mentions of the humours refer to the ancient Greek theory that a person's health and personality were determined by the balance of four basic fluids in the body: blood, phlegm, yellow bile and black bile. A dominance of any fluid would cause extremes in behaviour. An excess of blood created a sanguine person who was joyful, aggressive and passionate; a phlegmatic person was shy, fearful and sluggish; too much yellow bile led to a choleric temperament characterised by impatience, anger, bitterness and stubbornness; and excessive black bile created melancholy, a state of laziness, gluttony and lack of motivation. Literary treatment of the humours is exemplified by several characters in Ben Jonson's plays 'Every Man in His Humour' and 'Every Man out of His Humour'.

Ben Jonson

hymn

a song or ode of praise, usually addressed to gods, but sometimes to abstractions such as Truth, Justice, or Fortune.

hypallage

a type of hyperbaton involving an interchange of elements in a phrase or sentence so that a displaced word is in a grammatical relationship with another that it does not logically qualify.

hyperbaton

an inversion of the normal grammatical word order; it may range from a single word moved from its usual place to a pair of words inverted or to even more extremes of syntactic displacement. Specific types of hyperbaton are anastrophe, hypallage and hysteron proteron.

hyperbole

in literary criticism, deliberate exaggeration used to achieve an effect. In William Shakespeare's 'Macbeth', Lady Macbeth hyperbolises when she says, 'All the perfumes of Arabia could not sweeten this little hand'.

hypercatalectic

having an additional syllable after the final complete foot in a line of verse. A verse marked by hypercatalectic is called hypermetrical.

hypermetrical

a line, which contains a redundant syllable or syllables at variance with the regular metrical pattern.

hysteron proteron

related to the hyperbaton, a figure of speech in which the natural or logical order of events is reversed.

iamb

the most common metrical foot in English, German and Russian verse and many other languages as well; it consists of two syllables, a short or unaccented syllable followed by a long or accented syllable.

iambic pentameter

a metrical pattern in poetry which consists of five iambic feet per line. (An iamb, or iambic foot, consists of one unstressed syllable followed by a stressed syllable.)

ictus

the recurring stress or accent in a rhythmic or metrical series of sounds; also, the mark indicating the syllable on which such stress or accent occurs.

idealism

the artistic theory or practice that affirms the pre-eminent values of ideas and imagination, as compared with the faithful portrayal of nature in realism.

identical rhyme

see **perfect rhyme.**

ideology

the conscious or unconscious beliefs, habits and social practices of a particular society. These beliefs often seem true, correct and universal to members of that society when, in fact, they are relative and specific to that society. Ideology pervades every aspect of our lives, from our table manners to our politics; it is reflected in the clothes we wear, just as much as in our religious and educational practices. Within any society, ideologies are continually at odds or in conflict; however, certain ideologies are always dominant.

■ idiom

a word construction or verbal expression closely associated with a given language.

For example, in colloquial English, the construction 'how come' can be used instead of 'why' to introduce a question. Similarly, 'a piece of cake' is sometimes used to describe a task that is easily done.

■ idyll or idyl

a pastoral poem, usually brief, stressing the picturesque aspects of country life, or a longer narrative poem generally descriptive of pastoral scenes and written in a highly finished style.

■ image

a concrete representation of an object or sensory experience. Typically, such a representation helps evoke the feelings associated with the object or experience itself. Images are either 'literal' or 'figurative'. Literal images are especially concrete and involve little or no extension of the obvious meaning of the words used to express them. Figurative images do not follow the literal meaning of the words exactly. Images in literature are usually visual, but the term 'image' can also refer to the representation of any sensory experience.

In his poem 'The Shepherd's Hour', Paul Verlaine presents the following image: 'The Moon is red through horizon's fog;/ In a dancing mist the hazy meadow sleeps'. The first line is broadly literal, while the second line involves turns of meaning associated with dancing and sleeping.

■ imagery

the array of images in a literary work. Also, figurative language.

William Butler Yeats's 'The Second Coming' offers a powerful image of encroaching anarchy:

Turning and turning in the widening gyre
The falcon cannot hear the falconer;
Things fall apart....

■ imagism

a 20th century movement in poetry, advocating free verse, new rhythmic effects, colloquial language and the expression of ideas and emotions with clear, well-defined images, rather than through romanticism or symbolism.

■ imitation

see **mimesis.**

■ imperfect rhyme

see **near rhyme.**

■ impressionism

as applied to poetry, a late 19th century movement embracing imagism and symbolism, which sought to portray the effects (or poet's impressions), rather than the objective characteristics of life and events.

■ improvisatore

an improviser of verse, usually extemporaneously.

■ in medias res

a Latin term meaning 'in the middle of things'. It refers to the technique of beginning a story at its midpoint and then using various flashback devices to reveal previous action.

This technique originated in such epics as Virgil's 'Aeneid'.

■ incremental repetition

the repetition in each stanza—of a ballad, for example—of part of the preceding stanza, usually with a slight change in wording for effect.

■ induction

the process of reaching a conclusion, by reasoning, from specific premises to form a general premise. Also, an introductory portion of a work of literature, especially a play.

Geoffrey Chaucer's 'Prologue' to the Canterbury Tales, Thomas Sackville's 'Induction' to The Mirror of Magistrates and the opening scene in William Shakespeare's 'The Taming of the Shrew' are examples of inductions to literary works.

■ initiative

a primary consideration governing the process of composition, such as the meter selected for a poem; taken from Coleridge.

■ intentional fallacy

the belief that judgements of a literary work based solely on an author's stated or implied intentions are false and misleading. Critics who believe in the concept of the intentional fallacy typically argue that the work itself is sufficient matter for interpretation, even though they may concede that an author's statement of purpose can be useful.

Analysis of William Wordsworth's 'Lyrical Ballads', based on the observations about poetry he makes in his 'Preface' to the second edition of that work, is an example of the intentional fallacy.

■ interior monologue

a narrative technique in which characters' thoughts are revealed in a way that appears to be uncontrolled by the author. The interior monologue typically aims to reveal the inner self of a character. It portrays emotional experiences as they occur at both a conscious and unconscious level. Images are often used to represent sensations or emotions.

One of the best-known interior monologues in English is the Molly Bloom section at the close of James Joyce's 'Ulysses'. The interior monologue is also common in the works of Virginia Woolf.

■ interlocking rhyme

see **chain rhyme.**

internal rhyme

also called middle rhyme, a rhyme occurring within the line. The rhyme may be with words within the line but not at the line end, or with a word at the line end and a word within the line.

invective

see **lampoon.**

inversion

see **hyperbaton.**

invocation

see **apostrophe.**

ionic

a metrical foot of four syllables, either two long syllables followed by two short syllables (greater Ionic) or two short syllables followed by two long syllables (lesser Ionic); also, a verse or meter composed of Ionic feet.

Irish Literary Renaissance

a late nineteenth- and early twentieth-century movement in Irish literature. Members of the movement aimed to reduce the influence of British culture in Ireland and create an Irish national literature.

William Butler Yeats, George Moore and Sean O'Casey are three of the best-known figures of the movement.

irony

a literary device that uses contradictory statements or situations to reveal a reality that is different from what appears to be true. It is ironic for a firehouse to burn down, or for a police station to be burglarised. Verbal irony is a figure of speech that occurs when a person says one thing but means the opposite.

Sarcasm is a strong form of verbal irony that is calculated to hurt someone through, for example, false praise. Dramatic irony creates a discrepancy between what a character believes or says and what the reader or audience member knows to be true. Tragic irony is a form of dramatic irony found in tragedies such as 'Oedipus the King', in which Oedipus searches for the person responsible for the plague that ravishes his city and ironically ends up hunting himself.

Situational irony exists when there is an incongruity between what is expected to happen and what actually happens due to forces beyond human comprehension or control. The suicide of the seemingly successful main character in Edwin Arlington Robinson's poem 'Richard Cory' is an example of situational irony.

Edwin Arlington Robinson

Cosmic irony occurs when a writer uses God, destiny, or fate to dash the hopes and expectations of a character or of humankind in general. In cosmic irony, a discrepancy exists between what a character aspires to and what universal forces provide. Stephen Crane's poem 'A Man Said to the Universe' is a good example of cosmic irony, because the universe acknowledges no obligation to the man's assertion of his own existence.

■ isometric composition

the opposite of 'heterometric', i.e. verse that has lines all of the same number of feet.

■ Italian sonnet

see **sonnet.**

■ Italian sonnet

a fourteen-line verse form consisting of rhyme scheme a-b-b-a-a-b-b-a for the first 8 lines, followed by any rhyme scheme for the final 6 lines, so long as it consists of 3 rhyme pairs and it avoids a final rhymed couplet. (e.g. a-c-c-d-e-d-e)

■ Jack London (1876–1916)

Jack London, original name John Griffith London, was an American author. He was born in San Francisco. The illegitimate son of an astrologer and a Welsh farm girl, he had a poverty-stricken childhood. At 17, Jack London shipped as an able seaman to Japan and the Bering Sea. He was an oyster pirate, a gold-seeker in the first Klondike rush, a newspaper correspondent during the Russo-Japanese War and in 1914, a war correspondent in Mexico. His stories, romantic adventures with realistic setting and character, began to appear first in the Overland Monthly. In 1900, *The Son of the Wolf: Tales of the Far North* was published. Some of his other works are *The Sea-Wolf* (1904), *White Fang* (1905) and *Smoke Bellew* (1912). *Martin Eden* (1909) and *Burning Daylight* (1910) are partly autobiographical. *The People of the Abyss* (1903) and *The Iron Heel* (1907) are his most important works.

■ Jacobean age

the period of the reign of James I of England (1603-1625). The early literature of this period reflected the worldview of the Elizabethan Age, but a darker, more cynical attitude steadily grew in the art and literature of the Jacobean Age. This was an important time for English drama and poetry.

Milestones include William Shakespeare's tragedies, tragi-comedies and sonnets; Ben Jonson's various dramas, and John Donne's metaphysical poetry.

■ jargon

language that is used or understood only by a select group of people. Jargon may refer to terminology used in a certain profession, such as computer jargon, or it may refer to any nonsensical language that is not understood by most people.

Literary examples of jargon are Francois Villon's 'Ballades en jargon', which is composed in the secret language of the coquillards and Anthony Burgess's 'A Clockwork Orange', narrated in the fictional characters' language of 'Nadsat'.

Francois Villon

■ Jean Jacques Rousseau (1712–78)

Jean Jacques was a Swiss-French philosopher, author, political theorist and composer. Rousseau was born at Geneva, as the son of a watchmaker. His mother died shortly after his birth and his upbringing was haphazard. At 16, he set out on a wandering, that brought him into contact with Louise de Warens, who became his patron and later his lover. She arranged for his trip to Turin, where he became an unenthusiastic Roman Catholic convert.

In 1749, Rousseau won the first prize in a contest, held by the Academy of Dijon, on the question: 'Has the progress of the sciences and arts contributed to the corruption or to the improvement of human conduct?' Rousseau took the negative stand, contending that humanity was good by nature and had been fully corrupted by civilisation. His essay made him both famous and controversial. A second philosophical essay, *Discours sur l'origine de l'inégalité des hommes* (1754), is one of Rousseau's most mature and daring productions. He wrote the novel, *Julie, ou La Nouvelle Héloïse* in 1761. In his last years, he began *Rêveries du promeneur solitaire*, which was unfinished at the time of his death. He died at Ermenonville, near Paris. In its time, his epistolary novel *Héloïse* was immensely popular. *The Héloïse, Émile, the Confessions* and *the Rêveries* all transfer to the domain of literature and depict Rousseau's longing for closeness with nature.

■ James Dickey (1932-1997)

James Dickey was an American poet and novelist who also served in the air force during the World War II. Later on, he attended Vanderbilt University and graduated in 1946. He worked as an English teacher and an advertising executive. His poetry had great energy. He made use of the ordinary in his verse, joining the natural and mechanical on such topics as war, nature and machinery. *Into the Stone and Other Poems* (1960), *Buckdancer's Choice* (1965), *The Zodiac* (1976) and *Falling, May Day, Sermon* and *Other Poems* (1981) are some of the poems in his volume. His novel *Deliverance* (1969), in which a group of businessmen go on a hunting trip are forced to fight for their lives is probably his best known work. In 1972, he wrote the screenplay for the film, which was based on his novel *Deliverance*. His non-fiction works are *Self-Interviews* (1970) and several works of criticism.

■ James Joyce (1882–1941)

The most influential and significant Irish novelist of the 20th century was James Joyce. He was a master of the English language, exploiting all of its resources. His novel Ulysses, which is among the great works of world literature, utilises many radical literary techniques and forms.

Joyce was educated at Jesuit schools—Clongowes Wood College in Clane (1888–91) and Belvedere College in Dublin (1893–99)—and then attended University College in Dublin (1899–1902).

Joyce attempted to start a chain of motion picture theatres in Dublin and again in 1912 he engaged in an unsuccessful attempt to arrange for the publication of the short story collection *Dubliners*, which had to be abandoned due to fears of prosecution for obscenity and libel. A short volume of poetry, *Chamber Music*, was his first published volume, which appeared in 1907. He published two subsequent volumes of poetry, *Pomes Pennyeach* (1927) and *Collected Poems* (1937).

From 1922 until 1939, Joyce worked on Finnegans Wake (1939), a complex novel that attempts to connect multiple cycles of Irish and human history into the framework of a single night's events in the family of a Dublin publican. In 1931, Joyce finally married Nora. In 1941, Joyce died in Zürich after an operation for a perforated duodenal ulcer.

■ Jane Austen (1775–1817)

Jane Austen was a famous English novelist. She was the daughter of a clergyman. She wrote her first few novels, *Pride and Prejudice*, *Sense and Sensibility* and *Northanger Abbey* at Steventon, her father's Hampshire vicarage. On her father's retirement in 1801, the family moved to Bath for several years and then to Southampton, settling finally at Chawton Cottage, near Alton, Hampshire, which was Jane's home for the rest of her life.

The author's name did not appear on any of her title pages and although her own friends knew of her authorship, she received little public recognition in her lifetime.

Jane Austen's novels are comedies of manners that depict the self-contained world of provincial ladies and gentlemen. Most of her works revolve around the delicate business of providing husbands for marriageable daughters. Today, she is regarded as one of the great masters of the English novel.

■ jingle

a short poem marked by catchy repetition.

John Dryden (1631-1700)

John Dryden was an English poet, dramatist and critic. He was noticed for his Heroic Stanzas (1659), which was followed by his book *Astraea Redux*. In 1662, he was elected to the Royal Society. His long poem on the Dutch War, *Annus Mirabilis*, appeared in 1667. In 1668, he became poet laureate. He had a long and varied career as a dramatist. His most notable plays include the heroic dramas, *The Conquest of Granada* and *Aurenz-Zebe* (1675), *All for Love* (1677), a retelling of Shakespeare's Antony and Cleopatra and the comedy *Marriage à la Mode* (1672). His great political satire on Monmouth and Shaftesbury, Absalom and Achitophel, appeared in two parts (1681, 1682). *MacFlecknoe* (1682) and *Religio Laici* (1682) followed it. The preceding poems, as well as his Pindaric odes, *Alexander's Feast* and *Ode to the Memory of Mrs. Anne Killigrew*, place him among the most notable English poets. Throughout his life, he wrote brilliant critical prefaces, prologues and discourses, dealing with the principles of literary excellence. The best example is his *Essay of Dramatic Poesy* (1668). The last part of his life was occupied largely with translations from Juvenal, Vergil and others.

John Keats (1795-1821)

John Keats was one of the greatest English poets. His first volume of poems appeared in 1817. This volume included *I stood tip-toe upon a little hill, Sleep and Poetry* and the famous sonnet *On First Looking into Chapman's Homer.* In 1818, his long poem *Endymion* was published. The critical assaults of 1818 mark a turning point in Keats's life. The volume of poems which was published in 1820 contained some of the greatest works of Keats. It includes poems such as *Lamia, Isabella, The Eve of St. Agnes* and *Other Poems*. Keats is ranked, with Shelley and Byron, as one of the three great Romantic poets. His poems such as *Ode to a Nightingale, Ode on a Grecian Urn, To Autumn* and *Ode on Melancholy* are unequalled for dignity, melody and richness of sensuous imagery. *La Belle Dame sans Merci*, was one of his unparalleled works. Among his sonnets, familiar ones are *When I have fears that I may cease to be* and *Bright star! Would I were as steadfast as thou art. Lines on the Mermaid Tavern, Fancy* and *Bards of Passion and of Mirth* are delightful short poems. Some of Keats's finest work is in the unfinished epic *Hyperion*.

John Milton (1608-1674)

John Milton was one of the greatest poets of the English language. Milton wrote poetry in both Latin and English. In 1629, he wrote *On the Morning of Christ's Nativity L'Allegro* and *Il Penseroso.* In 1634, he wrote the masque *Comus* and wrote one of his greatest poems *Lycidas* in 1638. He wrote pamphlets like *Of Reformation in England* (1641) and *The Reason of Church Government Urged against*

Prelaty (1642). In 1649, he wrote *The Tenure of Kings and Magistrates,* which led to his securing position with Oliver Cromwell. He wrote his famous sonnet *Me thought I saw my late espoused saint,* in the memory of his second wife. His most famous work was *Paradise Lost* and *Paradise Regained.* These two epics are considered to be the greatest epics in the English literature. In these two great works, Milton's language is dignified and ornate, replete with biblical and classical allusions, allegorical representations, metaphors, puns and rhetorical flourishes. Milton wrote 18 sonnets in English and 5 in Italian. These sonnets follow the Petrarchan style and are regarded as the greatest ever written.

■ John Montague (1929)

John Montague is considered to be one of Ireland's best-known poets and writer. Montague developed interest in Irish poetry when he was just a schoolboy. His first poems were published in the 40s when he was a student at University College Dublin. He also wrote short stories and was a critic. His first collection *Poisoned Lands* came out in 1961 and soon after, he left Ireland for Yale on a Fulbright Fellowship. Some of his other published works *Hymn to the New Omagh Road* (1968) and *The Bread God* (1972) reflect his continued interest in Northern Ireland's affairs. He also wrote long poems and one of such poem was *The Rough Field,* which was published in 1972. In 1987, New York's then governor, Mario Cuomo, presented Montague with a citation for his literary achievements and contributions to the people of New York.

■ John Webster (158 –1634)

John Webster, an English playwright, was born in London. Very little is known of his life. But, there is evidence that shortly after 1600, he worked as one of a group of dramatists writing plays for the London theatre manager Philip Henslowe. The group included many talented playwrights, among them were Thomas Dekker, John Marston and Thomas Heywood, with each of whom Webster collaborated occasionally. Webster's reputation as a writer was first fully revealed in his great tragedies *The White Devil,* produced in 1612 and *The Duchess of Malfi*, staged about 1614. Violent and sensational, both plays treat the theme of revenge and generate a brooding, sombre mood. Both plays ensured Webster's longlasting critical acclaim and both are still produced. Despite their melodramatic themes, his soaring poetic dialogue and his grasp of human psychology redeem Webster's plays. Webster's highly poetic language and profound understanding of human suffering create a true tragic pathos and force.

■ Jonathan Swift (1667–1745)

Jonathan Swift was an English author, born in Dublin. He is widely recognised as one of the greatest satirists in the English language.

He was sent first to Kilkenny School and then to Trinity College, Dublin. In 1689, he became secretary to Sir William Temple at Moor Park, Surrey, where he formed his lifelong attachment to Esther Johnson, the *Stella* of his famous journal.

In 1708, he began a series of pamphlets on ecclesiastical issues with his ironic argument against abolishing Christianity. He joined the Tories in 1710, edited the Tory Examiner for a year and wrote various political pamphlets, notably *The Conduct of the Allies* (1711), *Remarks on the Barrier Treaty* (1712) and *The Public Spirit of the Whigs* (1714), in reply to Steele's Crisis. Swift became involved with another woman, Esther Vanhomrigh, the Vanessa of his poem Cadenus and Vanessa. Swift became a national hero of the Irish with his Drapier Letters (1724) and his bitterly ironical pamphlet *A Modest Proposal* (1729), which propounds that the children of the poor be sold as food for the tables of the rich. Swift's satirical masterpiece *Gulliver's Travels* appeared in 1726. In his last years, Swift was paralysed and afflicted with a brain disorder and by 1742, he was declared unsound of mind.

■ jongleur

a public entertainer in the Middle Ages who recited or sang chansons de geste, fabliaux and other poems, sometimes of their own composition, but more often those written by the trouvère.

■ Joseph Addison (1672-1719)

Joseph Addison was an English essayist, poet and statesman. The travels that he made to the Continent in 1699 to 1703 were recorded in Remarks on Italy (1705). Addison first achieved prominence with *The Campaign* (1704), this resulted in Addison's appointment in 1705 as undersecretary of state and in 1709 as secretary to the lord lieutenant of Ireland. He also held a seat in Parliament from 1708. Addison's greatest fame was his achievement as an essayist. His contributions raised technical perfection of the English essay to the heights never before achieved and perhaps never since surpassed He started his contributions to the Tatler in 1710. He continued writing for publications such as the *Spectator* (1711–12), *The Guardian* (1713) and *The New Spectator* (1714). In a prose style, he engaged men's thoughts toward reason, moderation and a harmonious life through simplicity, order and precision. His works also include an opera libretto, *Rosamund* (1707), a prose comedy, *The Drummer* (1716) and a neoclassical tragedy, *Cato* (1713). It was in his last years Addison achieved that greatest prominence. He was made secretary of state in 1717, an office he resigned the following year.

Joseph Brodsky

Joseph Brodsky was a Russian-American poet, who was a disciple of Anna Akhmatova. He began writing poetry in 1955. He was denounced by the Soviet government in 1963 and was exiled from the Soviet Union in 1972. Brodsky immigrated to the United States and started teaching at several colleges and built a reputation for himself as a distinguished literary figure. He wrote in English as well as in Russian.

His poetry is highly regarded for its formal technique, depth, intensity, irony and wit. The themes of his poems are often of loss and exile. *A Part of Speech*, *A volume of poetry*, *Less than On* and the posthumously published *On Grief and Reason* (1996), essays and the English-language poems of *To Urania* (1988) and *So Forth* (1996) are some of his best works. Later works include a play, *Marbles* (1989) and a book of prose, *Watermark* (1992). His Collected Poems in English was published in 2000.He-received MacArthur Award in 1981, a National Book Award in 1986 and many other honours. He won the Nobel Prize for Literature in 1987 and was poet laureate of the United States from 1991 to 1992.

Joseph Conrad (1857–1924)

He was originally named Jósef Teodor Konrad Walecz Korzeniowski. This English novelist was born in Berdichev, Russia (now Berdychiv, Ukraine). He is considered one of the greatest novelists and prose stylists in English literature. In 1874, Conrad went to sea and later joined (1878) an English merchant ship, becoming (1884) a master mariner as well as a British citizen. Retiring from the merchant fleet in 1894, he began his career as a novelist and all of his novels are written in English, an acquired language. His notable early works include *The Nigger of the Narcissus* (1897), *Lord Jim* (1900) and *the novellas Youth* (1902), *Heart of Darkness* (1902) and *Typhoon* (1903). The novels *Nostromo* (1904), *The Secret Agent* (1907), *Under Western Eyes* (1911) and *Chance* (1913) are regarded by many as Conrad's greatest works. Of his later works, *Victory* (1915) is the best known. He also collaborated on two novels with Ford Madox Ford, *The Inheritors* (1901) and *Romance* (1903). Conrad's novels combine realism and high drama. Their settings include nautical backgrounds as well as high society and international politics. Conrad was a skilled creator of atmosphere and character. He portrayed acutely the conflict between non-western cultures and modern civilisation. His characters exhibit the possibilities for isolation and moral deterioration in modern life.

Juvenalian satire

see **satire.**

■ **juxtaposition**

juxtapose is simply the placement of two things closely together to establish comparisons or contrasts.

■ **Kahlil or Khalil Gibran (1883-1931)**

Khalil Gibran was a Lebanese-American philosophical essayist, novelist, mystical poet and artist. He wrote in English and Arabic. Gibran's works were especially influential in the American popular culture in the 1960s. Gibran's early works were written in Arabic and from 1918 he published mostly in English. In 1920 he founded a society for Arab writers, Mahgar (al-Mahgar). He achieved lasting fame with such aphoristic, poetic works as *The Prophet* (1923) a book of 26 poetic essays, which has been translated into over 20 languages and *Jesus, the Son of Man* (1928). Some of his other famous works are *The Earth Gods* (1931), *Garden of the Prophet* (1933), *The Death of the Prophet* (1933), *Tears and Laughter* (1947) and *Nymphs of the Valley* (1948).

■ **kenning**

a compound word or phrase similar to an epithet, but which involves a multi-noun replacement for a single noun, such as 'wave traveller' for 'boat' or 'whale-path' for 'ocean' used especially in Old English, Old Norse and early Teutonic poetry. A type of periphrasis, some kennings are instances of metonymy or synecdoche.

■ **king's English**

the standard, pure or correct English speech or usage, also called Queen's English.

■ **knickerbocker group**

a somewhat indistinct group of New York writers of the first half of the nineteenth century. Members of the group were linked only by location and a common theme: New York life. Two famous members of the Knickerbocker Group were Washington Irving and William Cullen Bryant. The group's name derives from Irving's 'Knickerbocker's History of New York'.

William Cullen Bryant

■ **kunstlerroman**

see **bildungsroman.**

■ **lai**

a medieval narrative or lyric poem which flourished in 12th century France, consisting of couplets of five-syllable lines separated by single lines of two syllables. The number of lines and stanzas was not fixed and each stanza had only two rhymes, one rhyme for the couplets and the other for the two-syllable lines. Succeeding stanzas formed their own rhymes.

■ lake poets

see **lake school.**

■ lake school

These poets all lived in the Lake District of England at the turn of the nineteenth century. As a group, they followed no single 'school' of thought or literary practice, although their works were uniformly disparaged by the Edinburgh Review.

The poets of the Lake School were Robert Southey, William Wordsworth and Samuel Taylor Coleridge.

Also known as the Lake Poets.

Robert Southey

■ lampoon

a bitter, abusive satire in prose or verse attacking an individual. Motivated by malice, it is intended solely to reproach and distress.

■ language-centred poetry

where the forms of the words themselves are more significant than the sense or meanings of the words.

■ lay

a song or simple narrative poem. The form originated in medieval France. Early French *lais* were often based on the Celtic legends and other tales sung by Breton minstrels — thus the name of the 'Breton lay'. In fourteenth-century England, the term 'lay' was used to describe short narratives written in imitation of the Breton lays.

■ Leigh Hunt (1784-1859)

Leigh Hunt original name was James Henry Leigh Hunt. He was an English poet, critic and journalist. He was a friend of the eminent literary men of his time. With his brother John, Hunt established in 1808 the Examiner, a liberal weekly to which he contributed political articles. These articles were outspoken and were casting aspersions on the Prince Regent. Due to this the brothers were imprisoned from 1813 to 1815, but they continued to edit the journal from jail. In 1822, Hunt launched the Liberal with Shelley and Byron in Italy but it proved a failure. Hunt contributed to *The Indicator* (1819–21), *The Tatler* (1830–32) and Leigh Hunt's *London Journal* (1834–35). His literary fame rests chiefly on his miscellaneous light essays, his lyrics and his witty and informative autobiography. *The Story of Rimini* (1816) is his only long poem of consequence. He was noted for his dramatic and literary criticism. He praised Shelley and Keats very much.

■ leitmotiv

see **motif.**

■ leonine verse

named for a 12th century poet, Leonius, who first composed such verse, it consists of hexameters or of hexameters and pentameters in which the final syllable rhymes with one preceding the caesura, in the middle of the line.

■ Lewis Carroll (1832–98)

Lewis Carroll's original name was Charles Lutwidge Dodgson, an English writer, mathematician and an amateur photographer, was born near Daresbury, Cheshire (now in Halton). Educated at Christ Church College, Oxford, he was nominated to a studentship (life fellowship) in 1852 and he remained at Oxford for the rest of his life. He lectured in mathematics at Christ Church from 1855 until 1881. Among his mathematical works is *Euclid* and *His Modern Rivals* (1879). Carroll is chiefly remembered as the author of the famous children's books *Alice's Adventures in Wonderland* (1865) and its sequel, *Through the Looking Glass* (1872), both published under his pseudonym. He also wrote humorous verses, like the *Snark* (1876).

Carroll remained a bachelor all his life. Partly because of his stammer he found association with adults difficult and was most at ease in the company of children, especially little girls, with whom he was clearly obsessed. Early in 1856 he took up photography as a hobby, his photographs are still considered remarkable especially those of children.

■ lexical set

words that are habitually used within a given environment constitute a lexical set. Thus 'Monday, Tuesday, Wednesday...' form a lexical set.

■ lexis

the verbal 'texture' or rhetorical aspect of a work of literature, including the usual meanings of the terms 'diction' and 'imagery'.

■ light verse

a loose catch-all term describing poetry written with a relaxed attitude and ordinary tone on trivial, mundane, or frivolous themes. It is intended to amuse and entertain and is frequently distinguished by sophistication, wit, word play, elegance and technical competence. Among the numerous forms of light verse are clerihews, double dactyls, epigrams, limericks, nonsense poetry, occasional poetry, parodies, society verse and verse with puns or riddles.

limerick

a light or humorous verse form of five chiefly anapaestic verses of which lines one, two and five are of three feet and lines three and four are of two feet, with a rhyme scheme of aabba. The limerick, named for a town in Ireland of that name, was popularised by Edward Lear in his 'Book of Nonsense' published in 1846.

limited omniscience

see **point of view.**

line

a sequence of words printed as a separate entity on the page. In poetry, lines are usually measured by the number of feet they contain. The names for various line lengths are as follows: The number of feet in a line, coupled with the name of the foot, describes the metrical qualities of that line.

list poem

see **catalogue verse.**

literal language

an author uses literal language when he or she writes without exaggerating or embellishing the subject matter and without any tools of figurative language.

To say 'He ran very quickly down the street' is to use literal language, whereas to say 'He ran like a hare down the street' would be using figurative language.

literary ballad

see **ballad.**

literary symbol

see symbol.

literature

literature is broadly defined as any written or spoken material, but the term most often refers to creative works.

Literature includes poetry, drama, fiction and many kinds of non-fiction writing, as well as oral, dramatic and broadcast compositions not necessarily preserved in a written format, such as films and television programme.

litotes

a type of meiosis (understatement) in which an affirmative is expressed by the negative of the contrary.

lost generation

a term first used by Gertrude Stein to describe the post-World War I generation of American writers: men and women haunted by a sense of betrayal and emptiness brought about by the destructiveness of the war.

The term is commonly applied to Hart Crane, Ernest Hemingway, F. Scott Fitzgerald and others.

Hart Crane

■ **low comedy**

see comedy.

■ **low mimetic**

a mode of literature in which the characters exhibit a power of action which is roughly on our own level, as in most comedy and realistic fiction.

■ **lyric**

a type of brief poem that expresses the personal emotions and thoughts of a single speaker. It is important to realise, however, that although the lyric is uttered in the first person, the speaker is not necessarily the poet. There are many varieties of lyric poetry, including the dramatic monologue, elegy, haiku, ode and sonnet forms.

■ **lyric poetry**

a poem expressing the subjective feelings and personal emotions of the poet. Such poetry is melodic, since it was originally accompanied by a lyre in recitals. Most Western poetry in the twentieth century may be classified as lyrical.

A. E. Housman

Examples of lyric poetry include A. E. Housman's elegy 'To an Athlete Dying Young' the odes of Pindar and Horace, Thomas Gray and William Collins, the

Elizabeth Barrett Browning

sonnets of Sir Thomas Wyatt and Sir Philip Sidney, Elizabeth Barrett Browning and Rainer Maria Rilke and a host of other forms in the poetry

Christina Rossetti

of William Blake and Christina Rossetti, among many others.

■ **lyric verse**

one of the main groups of poetry, the others being narrative and dramatic. By far the most frequently used form in modern poetic literature; the term lyric includes all poems in which the speaker's ardent expression of a (usually single) emotional element predominates. Ranging from complex thoughts to the simplicity of playful wit, the power and personality of lyric verse is of far greater importance than the subject treated. Often brief, but sometimes extended in a long elegy or a meditative ode, the melodic imagery of skilfully written lyric poetry evokes in the reader's mind the recall of similar emotional experiences.

■ macaronic verse

originally, poetry in which words of different languages were mixed together or, more strictly, words in the poet's vernacular were given the inflectional endings of another language, usually for humorous or satiric effect. In modern times, however, in recognition of the multilingual relationships of sound and sense between different languages, it is used most often with serious intent, thus transformed from a species of comic or nonsense verse into poetry characterised by scholarly techniques of composition, allusion and structure.

■ madrigal

a short medieval lyric or pastoral poem expressing a simple delicate thought.

■ malapropism

a mistaken substitution of one word for another that sounds similar, generally with humorous effect, as in 'arduous romance' for 'ardent romance'.

■ mannerism

exaggerated, artificial adherence to a literary manner or style. Also, a popular style of the visual arts of late sixteenth-century Europe that was marked by elongation of the human form and by intentional spatial distortion. Literary works that are self-consciously high-toned and artistic are often said to be 'mannered'.

Authors of such works include Henry James and Gertrude Stein.

■ Marinism

excessive ornateness marked by the use of extravagant metaphors, so named from the 17th century Italian poet, Giambattista Marino and his school of followers.

Giambattista Marino

■ Mark Twain (1835–1910)

Mark Twain's original name was Samuel Langhorne Clemens. He was an American author, born in Florida, Mo. As humorist, narrator and social observer, Twain is unsurpassed in American literature. His novel *The Adventures of Huckleberry Finn* is a masterpiece of humour, characterisation and realism. It has been called the first modern American novel.

He first began writing for his brother's newspaper and later he worked as a printer in several major Eastern cities. He eventually began writing for the Virginia City Examiner and later was a newspaperman in San Francisco.

Soon, Mark Twain emerged a writer of tall tales and absurd anecdotes. He first won fame with the comic masterpiece *The Celebrated Jumping Frog of Calaveras County*.

In Hartford, Twain wrote some of his best work: *The Gilded Age* (1873), a satirical novel written with Charles Dudley Warner about materialism and corruption in the 1870s, two evocations of his boyhood in Hannibal, *The Adventures of Tom Sawyer* (1876) and *The Adventures of Huckleberry Finn* (1884), *The Prince and the Pauper* (1882), a novel for children.

His later life was shadowed by the deaths of two of his daughters and by the long illness and death of his wife in 1904.

■ Marxist criticism

an approach to literature that focuses on the ideological content of a work—its explicit and implicit assumptions and values about matters such as culture, race, class and power. Marxist criticism, based largely on the writings of Karl Marx, typically aims at not only revealing and clarifying ideological issues but also correcting social injustices. Some Marxist critics use literature to describe the competing socio-economic interests that too often advance capitalist interests such as money and power rather than socialist interests such as morality and justice. They argue that literature and literary criticism are essentially political because they either challenge or support economic oppression. Because of this strong emphasis on the political aspects of texts, Marxist criticism focuses more on the content and themes of literature than on its form.

■ Mary Wollstonecraft Shelley (1797–1851)

Mary Wollstonecraft, an English author was the daughter of William Godwin and Mary Wollstonecraft. She fell in love with the poet Percy Bysshe Shelley in 1814 and accompanied him abroad. After the death of his first wife in 1816, Shelley married Mary. Her most notable contribution to literature is her novel of terror, *Frankenstein*, published in 1818. It is the story of a German student who learns the secret of infusing life into inanimate matter and creates a monster that ultimately destroys him. Among her other novels are *Valperga* (1823), *The Last Man* (1826) and the partly autobiographical *Lodore* (1835). After Shelley's death in 1822, she devoted herself to caring for her aged father and educating her only surviving child, Percy Florence Shelley. She edited her husband's works in 1839–40.

masculine rhyme

a rhyme occurring in words of one syllable or in an accented final syllable, such as light and sight or arise and surprise.

masque

a lavish and elaborate form of entertainment, often performed in royal courts, that emphasises song, dance and costume. The Renaissance form of the masque grew out of the spectacles of masked figures common in medieval England and Europe. The masque reached its peak of popularity and development in seventeenth-century England, during the reigns of James I and, especially, of Charles I. Ben Jonson, the most significant masque writer, also created the 'antimasque' which incorporates elements of humour and the grotesque into the traditional masque and achieved greater dramatic quality.

Masque-like interludes appear in Edmund Spenser's 'The Faerie Queene' and in William Shakespeare's 'The Tempest'. One of the best-known English masques is John Milton's 'Comus'.

Matthew Arnold (1822-1888)

Matthew Arnold, an English poet and critic. Arnold was appointed inspector of schools in 1851. He went on a number of missions to European schools during his tenure. Educational systems on the Continent impressed him very much and he wrote several works about them. *The Strayed Reveller* (1849) was his first volume of poems and was followed by *Empedocles on Etna* (1852). His work *Poems* (1853) contained verse from the earlier volumes as well as new poems, including *The Scholar Gypsy* and *Sohrab and Rustum*. Its second series appeared in 1855 and was followed by *Merope: A Tragedy* (1858) and *New Poems* (1867). His verse exemplifies the romantic pessimism of the 19th century. Poems such as *Dover Beach* reflect his feelings of spiritual isolation. Arnold was among the most important literary critics of his age. From 1857 to 1867 he was Professor of Poetry at Oxford and at this time he started writing books on criticism, like *On Translating Homer* (1861), *Essays in Criticism* (1865, Ser. 2, 1888) and *On the Study of Celtic Literature* (1867). He included social criticism in *On Culture and Anarchy* (1869) His interest in religion can be seen in *St. Paul and Protestantism* (1870), *Literature and Dogma* (1873). He was the apostle of a new culture.

measure

the foot, verse, or time sequence used in a literary work, especially a poem. Measure is often used somewhat incorrectly as a synonym for Meter.

■ meiosis

an understatement; the presentation of a thing with under emphasis in order to achieve a greater effect.

■ meistersingers

members of various German trade guilds formed in the 15th and 16th centuries by merchants and craftsmen for the cultivation of poetry and music, succeeding the Minnesingers.

■ melic verse

capable of being sung. The term is derived from an ornate form of Greek lyric poetry of the 7th and 6th centuries B.C.

■ melodrama

a term applied to any literary work that relies on implausible events and sensational action for its effect. The conflicts in melodramas typically arise out of plot rather than characterisation; often a virtuous individual must somehow confront and overcome a wicked oppressor. Usually, a melodramatic story ends happily, with the protagonist defeating the antagonist at the last possible moment. Thus, melodramas entertain the reader or audience with exciting action while still conforming to a traditional sense of justice.

■ melos

the rhythm, movement and sound of words; the aspect of literature which is analogous to music and often shows some actual relation to it, derived from Aristotle's melopoia.

■ memoirs

an autobiographical form of writing in which the author gives his or her personal impressions of significant figures or events. This form is different from the autobiography because it does not centre on the author's own life and experiences.

Early examples of memoirs include the Viscount de Chateaubriand's 'The Memoirs of Chateaubriand' and Giacomo Casanova's 'History of My Life', while modern memoirs include reminiscences of World War II by Dwight Eisenhower, Viscount Montgomery and Charles de Gaulle.

Giacomo Casanova

■ mesostich

see **acrostic poem**.

■ metaphor

a metaphor is a figure of speech that makes a comparison between two unlike things, without using the word like or as. Metaphors assert the identity of dissimilar things, as when Macbeth asserts that life is a 'brief candle'. Metaphors can be subtle and powerful and can transform people, places, objects and ideas into whatever the writer imagines them to be.

An implied metaphor is a more subtle comparison; the terms being compared are not so specifically explained. For example, to describe a stubborn man unwilling to leave, one could say that he was 'a mule standing his ground'. This is a fairly explicit metaphor; the man is being compared to a mule. But to say that the man 'brayed his refusal to leave' is to create an implied metaphor, because the subject (the man) is never overtly identified as a mule. Braying is associated with the mule, a notoriously stubborn creature and so the comparison between the stubborn man and the mule is sustained. Implied metaphors can slip by inattentive readers who are not sensitive to such carefully chosen, highly concentrated language.

An extended metaphor is a sustained comparison in which part or all of a poem consists of a series of related metaphors. Robert Francis's poem 'Catch' relies on an extended metaphor that compares poetry to playing catch.

A controlling metaphor runs through an entire work and determines the form or nature of that work. The controlling metaphor in Anne Bradstreet's poem 'The Author to Her Book' likens her book to a child.

Synecdoche is a kind of metaphor in which a part of something is used to signify the whole, as when a gossip is called a 'wagging tongue' or when ten ships are called 'ten sails'. Sometimes, synecdoche refers to the whole being used to signify the part, as in the phrase 'Boston won the baseball game'. Clearly, the entire city of Boston did not participate in the game; the whole of Boston is being used to signify the individuals who played and won the game.

Metonymy is a type of metaphor in which something closely associated with a subject is substituted for it. In this way, we speak of the 'silver screen' to mean motion pictures, 'the crown' to stand for the king, 'the White House' to stand for the activities of the president.

■ metaphysical

of or relating to a group of 17th century poets whose verse was distinguished by an intellectual and philosophical style, with extended metaphors or conceits comparing very dissimilar things.

■ metaphysical conceit

see **conceit.**

■ metaphysical poetry

the body of poetry produced by a group of seventeenth-century English writers called the 'Metaphysical Poets'. The group includes John Donne and Andrew Marvell. The Metaphysical Poets made use of everyday speech, intellectual analysis and unique imagery. They aimed to portray the ordinary conflicts and contradictions of life. Their poems often took the form of an argument and many of them emphasise physical and religious love as well as the fleeting nature of life. Elaborate conceits are typical in metaphysical poetry.

Marvell's 'To His Coy Mistress' is a well-known example of a metaphysical poem.

■ **meter**

when a rhythmic pattern of stresses recurs in a poem, it is called meter. Metrical patterns are determined by the type and number of feet in a line of verse; combining the name of a line length with the name of a foot concisely describes the meter of the line. Rising meter refers to metrical feet which move from unstressed to stressed sounds, such as the iambic foot and the anapaestic foot. Falling meter refers to metrical feet which move from stressed to unstressed sounds, such as the trochaic foot and the dactylic foot. See also **accent, foot, iambic pentameter, line.**

■ **metonymy**

a figure of speech involving the substitution of one noun for another of which it is an attribute or which is closely associated with it, e.g., 'the kettle boils' or 'he drank the cup'. Metonymy is very similar to synecdoche.

■ **metrical pause**

a 'rest' or 'hold' that has a temporal value, usually to compensate for the omission of an unstressed syllable in a foot.

■ **metrical substitution**

small variations within a metrical pattern

■ **metrics**

the branch of prosody concerned with meter.

■ **middle diction**

see **diction.**

■ **middle rhyme**

see **internal rhyme.**

■ **miltonic**

pertaining to the poetry or style of the poet, John Milton, one of the most respected figures in English literature.

■ **mimesis**

literally, imitation or realistic representation –– but its poetic significance is more specific: it refers to the combination of sound in phonetic symbolism and onomatopoeia (sound suggestion) with the connotative, symbolic and synesthetic effects of the words themselves and their syntactic arrangement to resemble, reinforce, shape and temper their lexical sense in a manner that mirrors the meaning.

■ **minnesingers**

lyric poets of Germany in the 12th to 14th centuries, all men of noble birth who received royal patronage and who wrote mainly of courtly love. They were succeeded by the Meistersingers.

■ **minstrel**

in the Middle Ages, the general term for a performer who subsisted by reciting verse and singing, usually accompanied by a harp. Some minstrels were travelling entertainers; others were permanently employed by nobles.

■ **minstrelsy**

the art and occupation of minstrels; also, a collection of minstrel songs or a group of musicians or minstrels.

■ **mise en scene**

the costumes, scenery and other properties of a drama.

Herbert Beerbohm Tree was renowned for the elaborate mises en scene of his lavish Shakespearean productions at His Majesty's Theatre between 1897 and 1915.

■ **mixed metaphor**

a metaphor whose elements are either incongruent or contradictory by the use of incompatible identifications, such as 'the dog pulled in its horns' or 'to take arms against a sea of troubles'.

■ **mock-epic or mock-heroic**

a satiric literary form that treats a trivial or commonplace subject with the elevated language and heroic style of the classical epic.

■ **mode**

a conventional power of action assumed about the chief characters in fictional literature, or the corresponding attitude assumed by the poet toward his audience in thematic literature. Such modes tend to succeed one another in a historical sequence.

■ **modernism**

modern literary practices. Also, the principles of a literary school that lasted from roughly the beginning of the twentieth century until the end of World War II. Modernism is defined by its rejection of the literary conventions of the nineteenth century and by its opposition to conventional morality, taste, traditions and economic values.

Many writers are associated with the concepts of Modernism, including Albert Camus, Marcel Proust, D. H. Lawrence, W. H. Auden, Ernest

D. H. Lawrence

Hemingway, William Faulkner, William Butler Yeats, Thomas Mann, Tennessee Williams, Eugene O'Neill and James Joyce.

■ **modulation**

in poetry, the harmonious use of language relative to the variations of stress and pitch.

molossus

in Greek and Latin verse, a metrical foot consisting of three long syllables.

monad

a symbol in its aspect as a centre of one's total literary experience; related to Hopkins's term 'inscape' and to Joyce's term 'epiphany'.

monody

a poem in which one person laments another's death.

monologue

a composition, written or oral, by a single individual. More specifically, a speech given by a single individual in a drama or other public entertainment. It has no set length, although it is usually several or more lines long.

An example of an 'extended monologue' — that is, a monologue of great length and seriousness — occurs in the one-Act, one-character play 'The Stronger' by August Strindberg.

monometer

a line of verse consisting of a single metrical foot or dipody.

monorhyme

a poem in which all the lines have the same end rhyme.

monostich

a poem or epigram of a single metrical line.

monosyllable

a word of one syllable.

mood

the prevailing emotions of a work or of the author in his or her creation of the work. The mood of a work is not always what might be expected based on its subject matter.

The poem 'Dover Beach' by Mathew Arnold offers examples of two different moods originating from the same experience: watching the ocean at night. The mood of the first three lines —

The sea is calm tonight
The tide is full, the moon lies fair
Upon the straights....

is in sharp contrast to the mood of the last three lines —

And we are here as on a darkling plain
Swept with confused alarms of struggle and flight,
Where ignorant armies clash by night.

mora (pl. morae)

the minimal unit of rhythmic measurement in quantitive verse, equivalent to the time it takes to pronounce an ordinary or average short syllable; two morae are equivalent to a long syllable.

mosaic rhyme

a rhyme in which two or more words produce a multiple rhyme, either with two or more other words, as go for / no more, or with one longer word, as cop a plea / monopoly. It is usually used for comic effect.

motif

a theme, character type, image, Metaphor, or other verbal element that recurs throughout a single work of literature or occurs in a number of different works over a period of time.

For example, the various manifestations of the colour white in Herman Melville's 'Moby Dick' is a 'specific' motif, while the trials of star-crossed lovers is a 'conventional' motif from the literature of all periods.

Also known as Motiv or Leitmotiv.

■ motiv

see **motif.**

■ motivated action

see **character.**

■ muckrakers

an early twentieth-century group of American writers. Typically,

Upton Sinclair

their works exposed the wrongdoings of big business and government in the United States.

Upton Sinclair's 'The Jungle' exemplifies the muckraking novel.

■ Munshi Premchand (1880-1936)

Premchand was pseudonym of Hindi writer Dhanpatrai who was born on 31 July 1880 at Lamati near Varanasi. His early education was in a madarasa under a Maulavi, where he learnt Urdu. When he was studying in the ninth class he was married, much against his wishes. He was then fifteen. In 1919, while he was a teacher at Gorakhpur, he passed his B.A., with English, Persian and History. He had a second marriage with Shivarani Devi, a child-widow, who wrote a book on him, Premchand ghar mein after his death.

Premchand's literary career started as a freelancer in Urdu. *Soz-e-Watan*, a collection of stories published by Premchand in 1907, attracted the attention of the British government. Premchand was the first Hindi author to introduce realism in his writings.

Premchand was a prolific writer. He has left behind a dozen novels and nearly 250 short stories. *Seva Sadan* was his first novel. His best-known novels are *Sevasadan, Rangamanch, Ghaban, Nirmala* and *Godan.* Besides being a great novelist, Premchand was also a social reformer and thinker. His greatness lies in the fact that his writings embody social purpose and social criticism rather than mere entertainment. In 1936 this renowned writer died.

■ muse

a source of inspiration, a guiding genius.

■ muses

nine Greek mythological goddesses, the daughters of Zeus and Mnemosyne (Memory). Each muse patronised a specific area of the liberal arts and sciences. Calliope presided over epic poetry, Clio over history, Erato over love poetry, Euterpe over music or Lyric Poetry, Melpomene over tragedy, Polyhymnia over hymns to the gods, Terpsichore over dance, Thalia over Comedy and Urania over astronomy. Poets and writers traditionally made appeals to the Muses for inspiration in their work.

John Milton invokes the aid of a muse at the beginning of the first book of his 'Paradise Lost':

Of Man's First disobedience and the Fruit
of the Forbidden Tree, whose mortal taste
Brought Death into the World and all our woe,
With loss of Eden, till one greater Man
Restore us and regain the blissful Seat,
Sing Heav'nly Muse, that on the secret top
of Oreb, or of Sinai, didst inspire
That Shepherd, who first taught the chosen Seed,
In the Beginning how the Heav'ns and Earth
Rose out of Chaos....

■ mystery

see suspense.

■ myth

an anonymous tale emerging from the traditional beliefs of a culture or social unit. Myths use supernatural explanations for natural phenomena. They may also explain cosmic issues like creation and death. Collections of myths, known as mythologies, are common to all cultures and nations, but the best-known myths belong to the Norse, Roman and Greek mythologies.

A famous myth is the story of Arachne, an arrogant young girl who challenged a goddess, Athena, to a weaving contest; when the girl won, Athena was enraged and turned Arachne into a spider, thus explaining the existence of spiders.

■ mythological criticism

an approach to literature that seeks to identify what in a work creates deep universal responses in readers, by paying close attention to the hopes, fears and expectations of entire cultures. Mythological critics (sometimes called archetypal critics) look for underlying, recurrent patterns in literature that reveal universal meanings and basic human experiences for readers regardless of when and where they live. These critics attempt to explain how archetypes (the characters, images and themes that symbolically embody universal meanings and experiences) are embodied in literary works in order to make larger connections that explain a particular work's lasting appeal. Mythological critics may specialise in areas such as classical literature, philology, anthropology, psychology and cultural history, but they all emphasise the assumptions and values of various cultures.

mythos

the narrative of a work of literature, considered as the grammar or order of words (literal narrative), plot or 'argument' (descriptive narrative), secondary imitation of action (formal narrative), imitation of generic and recurrent action or ritual (archetypal narrative), or imitation of the total conceivable action of an omnipotent God or human society (anagogic narrative). One of the four archetypal narratives, classified as comic, romantic, tragic and ironic.

nagoge or anagogy

the spiritual or mystical interpretation of a word or passage beyond the literal, allegorical or moral sense.

naive

primitive or popular, in the sense given those terms of an ability to communicate in time and space more readily than other types of literature.

narration

the telling of a series of events, real or invented. A narration may be either a simple narrative, in which the events are recounted chronologically, or a narrative with a plot, in which the account is given in a style reflecting the author's artistic concept of the story. Narration is sometimes used as a synonym for 'storyline'.

The recounting of scary stories around a campfire is a form of narration.

narrative

a verse or prose accounting of an event or sequence of events, real or invented. The term is also used as an adjective in the sense 'method of narration'. For example, in literary criticism, the expression 'narrative technique' usually refers to the way the author structures and presents his or her story.

Narratives range from the shortest accounts of events, as in Julius Caesar's remark, 'I came, I saw, I conquered' to the longest historical or biographical works, as in Edward Gibbon's 'The Decline and Fall of the Roman Empire', as well as diaries, travelogues, novels, ballads, epics, short stories and other fictional forms.

narrative poem

a poem that tells a story. A narrative poem may be short or long and the story it relates may be simple or complex.

narrative poetry

a non-dramatic poem in which the author tells a story. Such poems may be of any length or level of complexity.

Epics such as 'Beowulf' and ballads are forms of narrative poetry.

narrator

the voice of the person telling the story, not to be confused with the author's voice. With a first-person narrator, the I in the story present the point of view of only one character. The reader is restricted to the perceptions, thoughts and feelings of that single character. For example, in Melville's 'Bartleby, the Scrivener' the lawyer is the first-person narrator of the story. First-person narrators can play either a major or a minor role in the story they are telling. An unreliable narrator reveals an interpretation of events that is somehow different from the author's own interpretation of those events.

Often, the unreliable narrator's perception of plot, characters and setting becomes the actual subject of the story, as in Melville's 'Bartleby', the 'Scrivener'. Narrators can be unreliable for a number of reasons, they might lack self-knowledge (like Melville's lawyer), they might be inexperienced, they might even be insane. Naive narrators are usually characterised by youthful innocence, such as Mark Twain's 'Huck Finn' or J. D. Salinger's 'Holden Caulfield'.

An omniscient narrator is an all-knowing narrator who is not a character in the story and who can move from place to place and pass back and forth through time, slipping into and out of characters as no human being possibly could in real life. Omniscient narrators can report the thoughts and feelings of the characters, as well as their words and actions. The narrator of 'The Scarlet Letter' is an omniscient narrator.

Editorial omniscience refers to an intrusion by the narrator in order to evaluate a character for a reader, as when the narrator of 'The Scarlet Letter' describes Hester's relationship to the Puritan community. Narration that allows the characters' actions and thoughts to speak for themselves is called neutral omniscience.

Mark Twain

Most modern writers use neutral omniscience so that readers can reach their own conclusions. Limited omniscience occurs when an author restricts a narrator to the single perspective of either a major or minor character. The way people, places and events appear to that character is the way they appear to the reader.

Sometimes a limited omniscient narrator can see into more than one character, particularly in a work that focuses on two characters alternately from one chapter to the next. Short stories, however, are frequently limited to a single character's point of view. See also **persona, point of view** and **stream-of-consciousness technique**.

Naturalism

a literary movement of the late nineteenth and early twentieth centuries. The movement's major theorist, French novelist Emile Zola, envisioned a type of fiction that would examine human life with the objectivity of scientific inquiry. The Naturalists typically viewed human beings as either the products of 'biological determinism' ruled by hereditary instincts and engaged in an endless struggle for survival, or as the products of 'socio-economic determinism' ruled by social and economic forces beyond their control. In their works, the Naturalists generally ignored the highest levels of society and focused on degradation: poverty, alcoholism, prostitution, insanity and disease.

Thomas Hardy

Naturalism influenced authors throughout the world, including Henrik Ibsen and Thomas Hardy. In the United States, in particular, Naturalism had a profound impact. Among the authors who embraced its principles are Theodore Dreiser, Eugene O'Neill, Stephen Crane, Jack London and Frank Norris.

near rhyme

also called approximate rhyme, slant rhyme, off rhyme, imperfect rhyme or half rhyme, a rhyme in which the sounds are similar, but not exact, as in home and come or close and lose. Most near rhymes are types of consonance.

Negritude

a literary movement based on the concept of a shared cultural bond on the part of black Africans, wherever they may be in the world. It traces its origins to the former French colonies of Africa and the Caribbean. Negritude poets, novelists and essayists generally stress four points in their writings: One, black alienation from traditional African culture can lead to feelings of inferiority. Two, European colonialism and Western education should be resisted. Three, black Africans should seek to affirm and define their own identity. Four, African culture can and should be reclaimed. Many Negritude writers also claim that blacks can make unique contributions to the world, based on a heightened appreciation of nature, rhythm and human emotions — aspects of life they say are not so highly valued in the materialistic and rationalistic West.

Examples of Negritude literature include the Poetry of both Senegalese Leopold Senghor in 'Hosties noires' and Martiniquais Aime-Fernand Cesaire in 'Return to My Native Land'.

Negro renaissance

see **harlem renaissance.**

neoclassical period

see **neoclassicism.**

neoclassicism

in literary criticism, this term refers to the revival of the attitudes and styles of expression of classical literature. It is generally used to describe a period in European history beginning in the late seventeenth century and lasting until about 1800. In its purest form, Neoclassicism marked a return to order, proportion, restraint, logic, accuracy and decorum. In England, where Neoclassicism perhaps was most popular, it reflected the influence of seventeenth-century French writers, especially dramatists. Neoclassical writers typically reacted against the intensity and enthusiasm of the Renaissance period. They wrote works that appealed to the intellect, using elevated language and classical literary forms such as satire and the ode. Neoclassical works were often governed by the classical goal of instruction.

Joseph Addison

English neo-classicists included Alexander Pope, Jonathan Swift, Joseph Addison, Sir Richard Steele, John Gay and Matthew Prior; French neo-classicists included Pierre Corneille and Jean-Baptiste Moliere.

neoclassicists

see neoclassicism.

neologism

the use of new words or new meanings for old words not yet included in standard definitions, as in the recent application of the word 'cool' to denote, very good, excellent or fashionable. Some disappear from usage, others like 'hip' and 'feedback', for example, remain in the language.

neutral omniscience

see **narrator.**

new criticism

a movement in literary criticism, dating from the late 1920s, that stressed close textual analysis in the interpretation of works of literature. The New Critics saw little merit in historical and biographical analysis. Rather, they aimed to examine the text alone, free from the question of how external events — biographical or otherwise — may have helped shape it.

This predominantly American school was named 'New Criticism' by one of its practitioners, John Crowe Ransom. Other important New Critics included Allen Tate, R. P. Blackmur, Robert Penn Warren and Cleanth Brooks.

John Crowe Ransom

new historicism

an approach to literature that emphasises the interaction between the historic context of the work and a modern reader's understanding and interpretation of the work. New historicists attempt to describe the culture of a period by reading many different kinds of texts and paying close attention to many different dimensions of a culture, including political, economic, social and aesthetic concerns. They regard texts not simply as a reflection of the culture that produced them but also as productive of that culture playing an active role in the social and political conflicts of an age. New historicism acknowledges and then explores various versions of 'history' sensitising us to the fact that the history on which we choose to focus is coloured by being reconstructed from our present circumstances.

new Negro movement

see harlem renaissance.

Niccolò Machiavelli (1469–1527)

Niccolò Machiavelli was not only an Italian author and statesman but was one of the outstanding figures of the Renaissance. He was born in Florence.

A member of the impoverished branch of a distinguished family, he entered (1498) the political service of the Florentine republic and rapidly gained importance. As the defense secretary, he substituted (1506) a citizens' militia for the mercenary system then prevailing in Italy. Machiavelli became acquainted with power politics through his important diplomatic missions.

Machiavelli's best-known work, *Il principe* (1532), describes the means by which a prince may gain and maintain his power. The Prince and the Discourses show clearly Machiavelli's republican principles, which are also reflected in his *Istorie Fiorentine* (1532), a historical and literary masterpiece, entirely modern in concept.

Other works include *Dell'arte della guerra* (1521), which viewed military problems in relation to politics. He also wrote many poems and plays, notably the lively and ribald comedy *Mandragola* (1524). The chief works of Machiavelli are available in several popular English editions.

noble savage

the idea that primitive man is noble and good but becomes evil and corrupted as he becomes civilised. The concept of the noble savage originated in the Renaissance period but is more closely identified with such later writers as Jean-Jacques Rousseau and Aphra Behn.

Aphra Behn

First described in John Dryden's play 'The Conquest of Granada', the noble savage is portrayed by the various Native Americans in James Fenimore Cooper's 'Leatherstocking Tales' by Queequeg, Daggoo and Tashtego in Herman Melville's 'Moby Dick' and by John the Savage in Aldous Huxley's 'Brave New World'.

John Dryden

nonce word

from the expression, for the nonce, a word coined or used for a special circumstance or occasion only.

nonsense poetry

poetry which is absurd, foolish or preposterous, usually written in a catchy meter with strong rhymes. It often contains neologisms or portmanteau words.

normative rhyme

the duplication, at the ends of two or more lines of a given poem, of some of the sounds in the last stressed syllable of those lines, plus duplication of all the sounds in any weakly stressed syllables that might follow the stressed syllable. The vowel of the stressed syllable and any consonant sound that might follow it, must be the same in both rhyming words. But the consonant sound that precedes the vowel of the stressed syllable should be different on each rhyming word, e.g., 'so/go', 'round/abound', 'lotion/motion', but not 'relate/late'.

novel

a long fictional narrative written in prose, which developed from the novella and other early forms of narrative. A novel is usually organised under a plot or theme with a focus on character development and action.

The novel emerged as a fully

Samuel Richardson

evolved literary form in the mid-eighteenth century in Samuel Richardson's 'Pamela; or, Virtue Rewarded'.

■ novel of ideas

a novel in which the examination of intellectual issues and concepts takes precedence over characterisation or a traditional storyline.

Examples of novels of ideas include Aldous Huxley's 'Crome Yellow', 'Point Counter Point' and 'After Many a Summer'.

■ novel of manners

a novel that examines the customs and mores of a cultural group.

The novels of Jane Austen and Edith Wharton are widely considered novels of manners.

Jane Austen

■ novella

an Italian term meaning 'story'. This term has been especially used to describe fourteenth-century Italian tales, but it also refers to modern short novels.

The tales comprising Giovanni Boccaccio's 'Decameron' are examples of the novella. Modern novellas include Leo Tolstoy's 'The Death of Ivan Ilich', Fyodor Dostoyevsky's 'Notes from the Underground', Joseph Conrad's 'Heart of Darkness' and Henry James's 'The Aspern Papers'.

Joseph Conrad

numen

a spiritual source or influence, often identified with a natural object, phenomenon or place.

nursery rhyme

a short poem for children written in rhyming verse and handed down in folklore.

O. Henry (1862–1910)

O. Henry's original name was William Sydney Porter. He was an American short-story writer who was born in Greensboro, N.C. He went to Texas in 1882 and worked at various jobs—as teller in an Austin bank (1891–94) and as a newspaperman for the Houston Post. In 1898 an unexplained shortage in the Austin bank was charged to him. Although many people believed him innocent, he fled to the Honduras but returned to be with his wife, who was fatally ill. He eventually ended up in prison for three years, where he first started writing short stories. Upon his release, he settled in New York City and became a highly successful and prolific contributor to various magazines. His short, simple stories are noted for their careful plotting, ironic coincidences and surprise endings. Although his stories have been criticised as shallow and contrived. O. Henry did catch the colour and movement of the city and evidenced a genuine sympathy for ordinary people. His approximately 300 stories are collected in *Cabbages and Kings* (1904), *The Four Million* (1906), *The Voice of the City* (1908), *Options* (1909) and others.

objective correlative

an outward set of objects, a situation, or a chain of events corresponding to an inward experience and evoking this experience in the reader. The term frequently appears in modern criticism in discussions of authors' intended effects on the emotional responses of readers.

This term was originally used by T. S. Eliot in his 1919 essay 'Hamlet'.

objectivism

a type of 20th century poetry in which objects are selected and portrayed for their own particular value, rather than their symbolic quality or the intellectual concept of the author.

objectivity

a quality in writing characterised by the absence of the author's opinion or feeling about the subject matter. Objectivity is an important factor in criticism.

The novels of Henry James and, to a certain extent, the poems of John Larkin demonstrate objectivity and it is central to John Keats's concept of 'negative capability'. Critical and journalistic writing usually are or attempt to be objective.

John Larkin

occasional poem

a poem written for a particular occasion, such as a dedication, birthday, or victory. The encomium, elegy, prothalamium and epithalamium are examples of occasional poems.

occasional verse

poetry written on the occasion of a significant historical or personal event. Vers de societe is sometimes called occasional Verse although it is of a less serious nature.

Famous examples of occasional verse include Andrew Marvell's 'Horatian ode upon Cromwell's Return from England' Walt Whitman's 'When Lilacs Last in the Dooryard Bloom'd' — written upon the death of Abraham Lincoln — and Edmund Spenser's commemoration of his wedding, 'Epithalamion'.

Abraham Lincoln

octameter

a line of verse consisting of eight metrical feet.

octave

a poem or stanza composed of eight lines. The term octave most often represents the first eight lines of a Petrarchan sonnet.

An example of an octave is taken from a translation of a Petrarchan sonnet by Sir Thomas Wyatt:

The pillar perisht is whereto I leant,
The strongest stay of mine unquiet mind;
The like of it no man again can find,
From East to West Still seeking though he went.
To mind unhap! for hap away hath rent
Of all my joy the very bark and rind;
And I, alas, by chance am thus assigned
Daily to mourn till death do it relent.

octosyllable

a metrical line of eight syllables, such as iambic, tetrameter, or a poem composed of eight-syllable lines.

ode

name given to an extended lyric poem characterised by exalted emotion and dignified style. An ode usually concerns a single, serious theme. Most odes, but not all, are addressed to an object or individual. Odes are distinguished from other lyric poetic forms by their complex rhythmic and stanzaic patterns.

An example of this form is John Keats's 'Ode to a Nightingale'.

■ odeon or odeum

a small roofed theatre in ancient antiquity devoted to the presentation of musical and poetic works to the public in competition for prizes.

■ oedipus complex

a son's amorous obsession with his mother. The phrase is derived from the story of the ancient Theban hero Oedipus, who unknowingly killed his father and married his mother.

Literary occurrences of the Oedipus complex include Andre Gide's 'Oedipe' and Jean Cocteau's 'La Machine infernale', as well as the most famous, Sophocles' 'Oedipus Rex'.

Andre Gide

■ off rhyme

a near rhyme, such as 'down/noon', 'seat/fate'

■ Ogden Nash (1902-1971)

Ogden Nash, American poet, born in New York and studied at Harvard. He started writing advertising copy for *Doubleday, Page Publishing, New York* in 1925. He wrote plays and children's books. His first children book *The Cricket of Caradon* was published in 1925. He was popular for a wide assortment of immensely quotable verses, ranging from urbane satire to absurdity in their subject and rhyme. His first poem *Spring Comes to Murray Hills* was published in New York magazine in 1930. His collections include *Hard Lines* (1931), *I'm a Stranger Here Myself* (1938), *Selected Verse* (1946), *Versus* (1949), *The Private Dining Room* (1953), *You Can't Get There from Here* (1957), *Verses From 1929 On* (1959), *Everyone But Thee and Me* (1962) and *Bed Riddance* (1970).

■ Omar Khayyam

Omar Khayyam, a Persian poet and mathematician. He flourished around the 11th century. He got his last name because of his father's occupation. He was an astronomer under Sultan Malik Shah and undertook the task to reform the calendar. This work of Khayyam led to the adoption of a new era, the so-called Jalalian or Seljuk era. He wrote a number of important mathematical studies. In the west he was popular for his *Rubaiyat*, epigrammatic verse quatrains. His work was not famous in Europe until Edward FitzGerald first published the freely paraphrased English translation of them in 1859. The translation in English led to his influences even among native speakers of Persian. FitzGerald omitted many of the quatrains and rearranged them into a unity expressing his conception of Omar's philosOphy. Khayyam's verses often masks his serious reflections on metaphysical issues. In literally hundreds of editions his verses have been offered.

■ omniscience

see **point of view.**

■ omniscient narrator

see **narrator.**

■ one-act play

a play that takes place in a single location and unfolds as one continuous action. The characters in a one-act play are presented economically and the action is sharply focused.

■ onomatopoeia

the use of words whose sounds express or suggest their meaning. In its simplest sense, onomatopoeia may be represented by words that mimic the sounds they denote such as 'hiss' or 'meow'. At a more subtle level, the pattern and rhythm of sounds and rhymes of a line or poem may be onomatopoeic.

A celebrated example of onomatopoeia is the repetition of the word 'bells' in Edgar Allan Poe's poem 'The Bells'.

■ open couplet

a couplet of the Romantic period with run-on lines, in which the thought was carried beyond the rhyming lines of the couplet.

■ open form

sometimes called 'free verse' open form poetry does not conform to established patterns of meter, rhyme and stanza. Such poetry derives its rhythmic qualities from the repetition of words, phrases, or grammatical structures, the arrangement of words on the printed page, or by some other means. The poet E. E. Cummings wrote open form poetry; his poems do not have measurable meters, but they do have rhythm.

■ opera

a type of stage performance, usually a drama, in which the dialogue is sung.

Classic examples of opera include Giuseppi Verdi's 'La traviata' Giacomo Puccini's 'La Boheme' and Richard Wagner's 'Tristanund Isolde'. Major twentieth-century contributors to the form include Richard Strauss and Alban Berg.

■ operetta

a usually romantic comic opera.

John Gay's 'The Beggar's Opera', Richard Sheridan's 'The Duenna' and numerous works by William Gilbert and Arthur Sullivan are examples of operettas.

Richard Sheridan

opsis

the spectacular or visible aspect of drama; the ideally visible or pictorial aspect of other literature.

oral tradition

see **oral transmission.**

oral transmission

a process by which songs, ballads, folklore and other material are transmitted by word of mouth. The tradition of oral transmission predates the written record systems of literate society. Oral transmission preserves material sometimes over generations, although often with variations. Memory plays a large part in the recitation and preservation of orally transmitted material.

Breton lays, French fabliaux, national epics (including the Anglo-Saxon 'Beowulf', the Spanish 'El Cid' and the Finnish 'Kalevala'), Native American myths and legends and African folktales told by plantation slaves are examples of orally transmitted literature.

oration

formal speaking intended to motivate the listeners to some action or feeling. Such public speaking was much more common before the development of timely printed communication such as newspapers.

Famous examples of oration include Abraham Lincoln's 'Gettysburg Address' and Dr. Martin Luther King Jr.'s 'I Have a Dream' speech.

organic form

refers to works whose formal characteristics are not rigidly predetermined but follow the movement of thought or emotion being expressed. Such works are said to grow like living organisms, following their own individual patterns rather than external fixed rules that govern, for example, the form of a sonnet.

Oscar Wilde (1854–1900)

Oscar Wilde was pseudonym for Oscar Fingall O'Flahertie Wills Wilde. He was an Irish author and an intellectual, born in Dublin. He is most famous for his sophisticated, brilliantly witty plays, which were the first since the comedies of Sheridan and Goldsmith to have both dramatic and literary merit. He studied at Trinity College, Dublin and at Magdalen College, Oxford, where he distinguished himself for his scholarship and wit and also for his eccentricity in dress, tastes and manners. His first published work, *Poems* (1881), was well received. In 1884 he married Constance Lloyd and they had two sons, Cyril and Vyvyan. Later he began writing for and editing periodicals, but his active literary career began with the publication of *Lord Arthur Savile's Crime and Other Stories* (1891) and two collections of fairy tales, *The Happy Prince* (1888) and *The House of Pomegranates* (1892). In 1891 his novel *Picture of Dorian Grey* appeared. He also wrote two historical tragedies, *The Duchess of Padua* (1892) and *Salomé* (1893).

Oscar Wilde was charged with homosexual offences and sentenced to prison for two years. Released in 1897, he lived in France until his death, plagued by ill health and bankruptcy.

■ ottava rima

an eight-line stanza of Poetry composed in iambic pentameter (a five-Foot line in which each foot consists of an unaccented syllable followed by an accented syllable), following the abababcc rhyme scheme.

This form has been prominently used by such important English writers as Lord Byron, Henry Wadsworth Longfellow and W. B. Yeats.

Henry Wadsworth Longfellow

■ overstatement

see **hyperbole.**

■ Ovid (43 B.C.-A.D. 18)

Ovid's original name was Publius Ovidius Naso. He was a Latin poet. He enjoyed early and widespread fame as a poet and was known to the emperor Augustus. Ovid's poetry can be divided into three groups- erotic poems, mythological poems and poems of exile. He wrote 49 short poems many of which extol the charms of the poet's mistress Corinna, some of such love poems were *Amores, Epistulae heroidum* and *Ars amatoria.* In the mythological category are the Metamorphoses, a masterpiece and perhaps Ovid's greatest work. *The Fasti,* also a mythological poem, contains six books on the days of the year from January to June, giving the myths, legends and notable events called to mind on each day. The poems of exile include *Tristia* [sorrows], five books of short poems, conveying the poet's despair in his first five years of exile and his supplications for mercy and the *Epistulae ex Ponto* [letters from the Black Sea], in four books, addressed to friends in Rome, showing somewhat abated poetic power. He was a source of inspiration for the artists of the Renaissance and the baroque. He was a major influence in Europe.

■ oxymoron

a condensed form of paradox in which two contradictory words are used together, as in 'sweet sorrow' or 'original copy'. Oxymorons may be intentional or unintentional.

The following speech from William Shakespeare's 'Romeo and Juliet' uses several oxymorons:

Why, then, O brawling love! O loving hate!

O anything, of nothing first create!

O heavy lightness! serious vanity!
Mis-shapen chaos of well-seeming forms!
Feather of lead, bright smoke, cold fire, sick health!
This love feel I, that feel no love in this.

Pablo Neruda (1904-1973)

Neftalí Ricardo Reyes Basualto was original name of Pablo Neruda. He was a Chilean poet, diplomat and Communist leader. Neruda was a surrealist poet who revitalised everyday expressions and employed bold metaphors in free verse. His personal poetry brought him enormous acclaim and his poetry was filled with grief and despair and bespeaks a quest for simplicity. They proclaim the dramatic Chilean landscape and rage against the exploitation of the indigenous people. He exerted wide influence in Latin America through his writings and his political activities. His many volumes of poetry include *Crepusculario, Twenty Love Poems and One Song of Despair, Residence on Earth and Other Poems, Canto general, Elementary Odes, Nuevas odas elementals, A New Decade: 1958–1967, New Poems: 1968–1970* and *Toward the Splendid City*. Neruda was awarded the 1971 Nobel Prize in Literature during his service as Chilean ambassador to France

paean

a hymn of praise, joy, triumph, etc.

paeon

in ancient poetry, a metrical foot consisting of four syllables, one long and three short. The position of the long syllable can be varied in four ways, thus the foot can be called a primus, secundus, tertius or quartus paeon.

palindrome

a word, verse, or sentence in which the sequence of letters is the same forward and backward, as the word, 'madam', or the sentence, 'A man, a plan, a canal: Panama'. A variation in which the sequence of words is the same forward and backward is called a word-order palindrome.

palinode or palinody

a poem in which the poet contradicts or retracts something in an earlier poem.

panegyric

a speech or poem of elaborate praise for some distinguished person, object or event, similar to, but more formal than, an encomium.

pantheism

the idea that all things are both a manifestation or revelation of God and a part of God at the same time. Pantheism was a common attitude in the early societies of Egypt, India and Greece — the term derives from the Greek 'pan' meaning 'all' and 'theos' meaning 'deity'. It later became a significant part of the Christian faith.

William Wordsworth and Ralph Waldo Emerson are among the many writers who have expressed the pantheistic attitude in their works.

Ralph Waldo Emerson

pantoum

a poem in a fixed form, consisting of a varying number of 4-line stanzas with lines rhyming alternately; the second and fourth lines of each stanza are repeated to form the first and third lines of the succeeding stanza, with the first and third lines of the first stanza forming the second and fourth of the last stanza, but in reverse order, so that the opening and closing lines of the poem are identical.

parable

a story intended to teach a moral lesson or answer an ethical question.

In the West, the best examples of parables are those of Jesus Christ in the New Testament, notably 'The Prodigal Son' but parables also are used in Sufism, rabbinic literature, Hasidism and Zen Buddhism.

paradox

a statement that appears illogical or contradictory at first, but may actually point to an underlying truth.

'Less is more' is an example of a paradox. Literary examples include Francis Bacon's statement, 'The most corrected copies are commonly the least correct' and 'All animals are equal, but some animals are more equal than others' from George Orwell's 'Animal Farm'.

parallelism

a method of comparison of two ideas in which each is developed in the same grammatical structure. The repetitive structure lends wit or emphasis to the meanings of the separate clauses, thus being particularly effective in antithesis.

Ralph Waldo Emerson's 'Civilization' contains this example of parallelism: Raphael paints wisdom; Handel sings it, Phidias carves it, Shakespeare writes it, Wren builds it, Columbus sails it, Luther preaches it, Washington arms it, Watt mechanises it.

paraphrase

a prose restatement of the central ideas of a poem, in your own language.

parnassian

of or related to poetry, after Parnassus, a mountain in Greece with two summits; one summit was consecrated to Bacchus, the other to Apollo and the Muses, thus Parnassus was regarded as the seat of poetry and music.

■ parnassianism

a mid nineteenth-century movement in French literature. Followers of the movement stressed adherence to well-defined artistic forms as a reaction against the often-chaotic expression of the artist's ego that dominated the work of the Romantics. The Parnassians also rejected the moral, ethical and social themes exhibited in the works of French Romantics such as Victor Hugo. The aesthetic doctrines of the Parnassians strongly influenced the later symbolist and decadent movements.

Members of the Parnassian school include Leconte de Lisle, Sully Prudhomme, Albert Glatigny, Francois Coppee and Theodore de Banville.

■ parody

a humorous imitation of another, usually serious, work. It can take any fixed or open form, because parodists imitate the tone, language and shape of the original in order to deflate the subject matter, making the original work seem absurd. Anthony Hecht's poem 'Dover Bitch' is a famous parody of Matthew Arnold's well-known 'Dover Beach'. Parody may also be used as a form of literary criticism to expose the defects in a work. But sometimes parody becomes an affectionate acknowledgment that a well-known work has become both institutionalised in our culture and fair game for some fun. For example, Peter De Vries's 'To His Importunate Mistress' gently mocks Andrew Marvell's 'To His Coy Mistress'.

Andrew Marvell

■ paronomasia

a play on words in which the same word is used in different senses or words similar in sound are used in opposition to each other for a rhetorical contrast; a pun.

■ paronym

a word derived from or related to another word; also, the form in one language for a word in another, as in the English 'canal' for the Latin 'canalis'.

■ pasquinade

a lampoon or satirical writing.

■ pastiche

an artistic effort that imitates or caricatures the work of another artist.

■ pastoral

a term derived from the Latin word 'pastor' meaning shepherd. A pastoral is a literary composition on a rural theme. The conventions of the pastoral were originated by the third-century Greek poet Theocritus, who wrote about the experiences, love affairs and pastimes of Sicilian shepherds. In a pastoral, characters and language of a courtly nature are often placed in a simple setting. The term pastoral is also used to classify dramas, elegies and lyrics that exhibit the use of country settings and shepherd characters.

Percy Bysshe Shelley's 'Adonais' and John Milton's 'Lycidas' are two famous examples of pastorals.

■ pastoral elegy

see **elegy.**

■ pastoral poetry

poetry idealising the lives of shepherds and country folk, although the term is often used loosely to include any poems with a rural aspect.

■ pastorela

the Spanish name for the shepherds play, a folk drama re-enacted during the Christmas season.

Examples of pastorelas include Gomez Manrique's 'Representacion del nacimiento' and the dramas of Lucas Fernandez and Juan del Encina.

■ pastourelle

a form of pastoral poetry associated chiefly with French writers of the 12th and 13th centuries. Typically, the narrator, identified as a knight, recounts his love affair with a shepherdess.

■ pathetic fallacy

a term coined by English critic John Ruskin to identify writing that falsely endows nonhuman things with human intentions and feelings, such as 'angry clouds' and 'sad trees'.

The pathetic fallacy is a required convention in the classical poetic form of the pastoral elegy and it is used in the modern poetry of T. S. Eliot, Ezra Pound and the Imagists.

Also known as Poetic Fallacy.

Ezra Pound

■ pathos

an element in artistic expression evoking pity, sorrow or compassion.

■ rhyme royal

poetry in which the letters, words and lines are configured in such a way that the poem's printed appearance on the page forms a recognisable outline related to the subject, thus conveying or extending the meaning of the words.

■ pause

see **saesura and metrical pause.**

■ pelado

literally the 'skinned one' or shirtless one, he was the stock underdog, sharp-witted picaresque character of Mexican vaudeville and tent shows.

The pelado is found in such works as Don Catarino's 'Los effectos de la crisis' and 'Regreso a mi tierra'.

■ pen name

see **pseudonym.**

■ pentameter

a line of verse consisting of five metrical feet.

■ Percy Bysshe Shelley (1792-1822)

Percy Bysshe Shelley, an English poet. He is ranked as one of the great English poets of the Romantic Period. His first important poem, *Queen Mab*, privately printed in 1813, set forth a radical system of curing social ills by advocating the destruction of various established institutions. *Laon* and *Cynthna* appeared in 1817 but were withdrawn and reissued the following year as *The Revolt of Islam.* Shelley composed the great body of his poetry in Italy. *The Cenci*, a tragedy in verse exploring moral deformity, was published in 1819, followed by his masterpiece, *Prometheus Unbound* (1820). In 1821 *Epipsychidion* and his great elegy, *Adonais* was published. *Hellas*, a lyrical drama was published in 1822. His other poems include *Alastor* (1816) and the shorter poems *Ode to the West Wind, To a Skylark, Ozymandias, The Indian Serenade* and *When the Lamp Is Shattered.* His lyric poems are superb in their beauty, grandeur and mastery of language.

■ perfect rhyme

also called true rhyme or exact rhyme, a rhyme which meets the following requirements: (1) an exact correspondence in the vowel sound and, in words ending in consonants, the sound of the final consonant, (2) a difference in the consonant sounds preceding the vowel and (3) a similarity of accent on the rhyming syllable(s).

■ periphrasis

the substitution of an elaborate phrase in place of a simple word or expression, as 'fragrant beverage drawn from China's herb' for 'tea'.

■ persona

a Latin term meaning 'mask'. Personae are the characters in a fictional work of literature. The persona generally functions as a mask through which the author tells a story in a voice other than his or her own. A persona is usually either a character in a story who acts as a narrator or an 'implied author' a voice created by the author to act as the narrator for himself or herself.

Personae include the narrator of Geoffrey Chaucer's 'Canterbury Tales' and Marlow in Joseph Conrad's 'Heart of Darkness'.

■ personae

see **persona.**

■ personal point of view

see **point of view.**

■ persona literally

a persona is a mask. In literature, a persona is a speaker created by a writer to tell a story or to speak in a poem. A persona is not a character in a story or narrative, nor does a persona necessarily directly reflect the author's personal voice. A persona is a separate self, created by and distinct from the author, through which he or she speaks.

■ personification

a form of metaphor in which human characteristics are attributed to nonhuman things. Personification offers the writer a way to give the world life and motion by assigning familiar human behaviour and emotions to animals, inanimate objects and abstract ideas. For example, in Keats's 'Ode on a Grecian Urn', the speaker refers to the urn as an 'unravished bride of quietness'.

■ Petrarch (1304- 1374)

Petrarch or Francesco Petrarcah, an Italian poet and humanist. He was regarded as one of the greatest figures of Italian literature. He wrote numerous lyrics, sonnets and canzoni. His verses got him great fame and in 1341 he was crowned laureate at Rome. Petrarch's friendship with the republican Cola di Rienzi inspired the famous ode *Italia mia.* In his last years Petrarch enjoyed great fame and even after his death and ceremonial burial at Arquà his influence continued to spread. He was instrumental in spreading the Renaissance point of views. In his poetry he ignored medieval courtly conventions and defined true emotions. He also perfected the sonnet form and is considered by many to be the first modern poet. He influenced contemporary historiography through his epic Africa. He considered his *Trionfi* [triumphs] and the well-known lyrics of the *Canzoniere* [song book] less important than his Latin works, which include, besides *Africa, Metrical Epistles, On Contempt for the Worldly Life, On Solitude, Eclogues* and *the Letters.* Many writers copied his style, some of them were Chaucer, Spenser, Surrey and Wyatt. He was truly a great poet and reached great poetic heights in both tongues i.e. Itallian and Latin.

■ petrarchan sonnet

an Italian sonnet form perfected by Petrarch (1304-1374), characterised by an octave with a rhyme scheme of abbaabba and a sestet rhyming variously, but usually cdecde or cdccdc. The octave typically introduces the theme or problem, with the sestet providing the resolution.

■ **pharmakos**

the character in an ironic fiction who has the role of a scapegoat or arbitrarily chosen victim.

■ **phase**

one of the five contexts in which the narrative and meaning of a work of literature may be considered, classified as literal, descriptive, formal, archetypal and anagogic. One of six distinguishable stages of a mythos.

■ **phenomenology**

a method of literary criticism based on the belief that things have no existence outside of human consciousness or awareness. Proponents of this theory believe that art is a process that takes place in the mind of the observer as he or she contemplates an object rather than a quality of the object itself.

Among phenomenological critics are Edmund Husserl, George Poulet, Marcel Raymond and Roman Ingarden.

■ **phonetic symbolism**

sound suggestiveness; the association of particular word-sounds with common areas of meaning so that other words of similar sounds come to be associated with those meanings. Also called sound symbolism, it is utilised by poets to achieve sounds appropriate to their significance.

■ **picaresque**

the term applied to literature dealing sympathetically with the adventures of clever and amusing rogues.

■ **picaresque novel**

episodic fiction depicting the adventures of a roguish central character ('picaro' is Spanish for 'rogue'). The picaresque hero is commonly a low-born but clever individual who wanders into and out of various affairs of love, danger and farcical intrigue. These involvements may take place at all social levels and typically present a humorous and wide-ranging satire of a given society.

Prominent examples of the picaresque novel are 'Don Quixote' by Miguel de Cervantes, 'Tom Jones' by Henry Fielding and 'Moll Flanders' by Daniel Defoe.

■ **picture poem**

a type of open form poetry in which the poet arranges the lines of the poem so as to create a particular shape on the page. The shape of the poem embodies its subject; the poem becomes a picture of what the poem is describing. Michael McFee's 'In Medias Res' is an example of a picture poem.

Michael McFee

■ pierian

of or relating to learning or poetry, after the region of Pieria in ancient Macedonia which once worshipped the Muses.

■ pindaric verse

in Greek literature, a poem designed for song, of various meters and of lofty style, patterned after the odes of the classical Greek poet, Pindar. Though metrically complex and varying from one ode to another, Pindaric verse, also called Dorian or choric odes, regularly consists of a similarly-structured strophe and an antistrophe, followed by an epode of different length and structure.

■ plagiarism

claiming another person's written material as one's own. Plagiarism can take the form of direct, word-for-word copying or the theft of the substance or idea of the work.

A student who copies an encyclopaedia entry and turns it in as a report for school is guilty of plagiarism.

■ platonic criticism

a form of criticism that stresses an artistic work's usefulness as an agent of social engineering rather than any quality or value of the work itself.

Platonic criticism takes as its starting point the ancient Greek philosopher Plato's comments on art in his 'Republic'.

■ platonism

the embracing of the doctrines of the philosopher Plato, popular among the poets of the Renaissance and the Romantic period. Platonism is more flexible than Aristotelian Criticism and places more emphasis on the supernatural and unknown aspects of life.

Platonism is expressed in the love Poetry of the Renaissance, the fourth book of Baldassare Castiglione's 'The Book of the Courtier' and the poetry of William Blake, William Wordsworth, Percy Bysshe Shelley, Friedrich Holderlin, William Butler Yeats and Wallace Stevens.

Friedrich Holderlin

■ plausible action

see character.

■ play

see drama.

■ play on words

see **paronomasia, pun.**

playwright

see drama.

pleiad or pleiade

named after the open cluster in the constellation Taurus, a group of 16th century French poets who sought to restore the level of French poetry from its decline in the Middle Ages to classical standards as well as to enhance the richness of the French language.

pleonasm

redundancy; the use of more words than necessary to express the sense of a thing, but which often stress or enrich the thought, such as, 'I touched it with my own hands' or 'a tiny little acorn'.

ploce

the general term for a figure of speech in which a word or phrase is repeated in close proximity within a clause or line, usually for emphasis or for extended significance, as 'A wife who was a wife indeed' or 'there are medicines and medicines'.

plosive

a consonantal sound in the formation of which the passage of air is completely blocked, such as 'p', 'b', 't'. The blockage can be made in a variety of places (between the lips, between the tongue and teeth, between the tongue and palate). A 'bi-labial plosive' is made with the lips (Latin labia)

plot

an author's selection and arrangement of incidents in a story to shape the action and give the story a particular focus. Discussions of plot include not just what happens, but also how and why things happen the way they do. Stories that are written in a pyramidal pattern divide the plot into three essential parts. The first part is the rising action, in which complication creates some sort of conflict for the protagonist. The second part is the climax, the moment of greatest emotional tension in a narrative, usually marking a turning point in the plot at which the rising action reverses to become the falling action. The third part, the falling action (or resolution) is characterised by diminishing tensions and the resolution of the plot's conflicts and complications. In medias res is a term used to describe the common strategy of beginning a story in the middle of the action. In this type of plot, we enter the story on the verge of some important moment.

poem

in its broadest sense, a composition utilising rhyme, meter, concrete detail and expressive language to create a literary experience with emotional and aesthetic appeal.

Typical poems include sonnets, odes, elegies, haiku, ballads and free verse.

poems of chance

poetry created by adherents of the dadaistic movement, composed by writing down, without alteration, an illogical chance association of words, free of the limitations of rational and artistic thought processes.

■ poesy or poesie

a poem or a group of poems, i.e., poetry. The term also refers to the art of writing poems, often used in the sense of trite or sentimentalised poetic writing.

■ poet

an author who writes Poetry or Verse. The term is also used to refer to an artist or writer who has an exceptional gift for expression, imagination and energy in the making of art in any form.

Well-known poets include Horace, Basho, Sir Philip Sidney, Sir Edmund Spenser, John Donne andrew Marvell, Alexander Pope, Jonathan Swift, George Gordon, Lord Byron, John Keats, Christina Rossetti, W. H. Auden, Stevie Smith and Sylvia Plath.

Lord Byron

■ poet laureate

a poet honoured for his artistic achievement or selected as most representative of his country or area; in England, a court official appointed by the sovereign, whose original duties included the composition of odes in honour of the sovereign's birthday and in celebration of State occasions of importance.

■ poetaster

an inadequate writer of verses, an inferior poet.

■ poete maudit

a term derived from Paul Verlaine's 'Les poetes maudits (The Accursed Poets)', a collection of essays on the French symbolist writers Stephane Mallarme, Arthur Rimbaud and Tristan Corbiere. In the sense intended by Verlaine, the poet is 'accursed' for choosing to explore extremes of human experience outside of middle-class society.

The poete maudit is described in Charles Baudelaire's poem 'Benediction' from which Verlaine may have taken his title.

■ poetic diction

see **diction.**

■ poetic fallacy

see **pathetic fallacy.**

■ poetic justice

an outcome in a literary work, not necessarily a poem, in which the good is rewarded and the evil is punished, especially in ways that particularly fit their virtues or crimes.

For example, a murderer may himself be murdered, or a thief will find himself penniless.

poetic license

the liberties generally allowable for a poet to take with his subject-matter to achieve a desired effect or with his grammatical construction, etc., to conform to the requirements of rhyme and meter; but in a broader sense, it includes 'creative' deviations from historical fact, such as anachronisms.

poetics

this term has two closely related meanings. It denotes (1) an aesthetic theory in literary criticism about the essence of Poetry or (2) rules prescribing the proper methods, content, style, or diction of poetry. The term poetics may also refer to theories about literature in general, not just poetry.

poeticule

a dabbler in poetry; a poetaster.

poetry

in its broadest sense, writing that aims to present ideas and evoke an emotional experience in the reader through the use of meter, imagery, connotative and concrete words and a carefully constructed structure based on rhythmic patterns. Poetry typically relies on words and expressions that have several layers of meaning. It also makes use of the effects of regular rhythm on the ear and may make a strong appeal to the senses through the use of imagery.

Edgar Allan Poe's 'Annabel Lee' and Walt Whitman's 'Leaves of Grass' are famous examples of poetry.

poets' corner

a portion of the South Transept of Westminster Abbey, which contains the remains of many famous literary figures, including Chaucer and Spenser and also displays memorials to others who are buried elsewhere.

point of view

the narrative perspective from which a literary work is presented to the reader. There are four traditional points of view. The 'third person omniscient' gives the reader a 'godlike' perspective, unrestricted by time or place, from which to see actions and look into the minds of characters. This allows the author to comment openly on characters and events in the work. The 'third person' point of view presents the events of the story from outside of any single character's perception, much like the omniscient point of view, but the reader must understand the action as it takes place and without any special insight into characters' minds or motivations. The 'first person' or 'personal' point of view relates events as they are perceived by a single character. The main character 'tells' the story and may offer opinions about the action and characters, which differ from those of the author. Much less common than omniscient, third person and first person is the 'second person' point of view, wherein the author tells the story as if it is happening to the reader.

James Thurber employs the omniscient point of view in his short story 'The Secret Life of Walter Mitty'. Ernest Hemingway's 'A Clean, Well-Lighted Place' is a short story told from the third person point of view. Mark Twain's novel 'Huck Finn' is presented from the first person viewpoint. Jay McInerney's 'Bright Lights', 'Big City' is an example of a novel, which uses the second person point of view.

■ polemic

a work in which the author takes a stand on a controversial subject, such as abortion or religion. Such works are often extremely argumentative or provocative.

Classic examples of polemics include John Milton's 'Aeropagitica' and Thomas Paine's 'The American Crisis'.

■ polyphonic prose

a type of free verse using characteristic devices of verse such as alliteration and assonance, but presented in a form resembling prose.

■ polyptoton

a figure of speech in which a word is repeated in a different form of the same root or stem, as Shakespeare's 'Then thou, whose shadow shadows doth make bright' or repeated with its word class changed into a different part of speech, as Tennyson's 'My own heart's heart and my ownest own, farewell'.

■ polyrhythmic verse

a type of free verse characterised by a variety of rhythms, often non-integrated or contrasting.

■ polysyllable

a word consisting of several syllables. It is most often applied to words of more than three syllables.

■ polysyndeton

the repetition of a number of conjunctions in close succession, as in, 'We have men **and** arms **and** planes **and** tanks'.

■ pornography

writing intended to provoke feelings of lust in the reader. Such works are often condemned by critics and teachers, but those which can be shown to have literary value are viewed less harshly.

Literary works that have been described as pornographic include Ovid's 'The Art of Love', Margaret of Angouleme's 'Heptameron', John Cleland's 'Memoirs of a Woman of Pleasure'; or, 'the Life of Fanny Hill', the anonymous 'My Secret Life', D. H. Lawrence's 'Lady Chatterley's Lover' and Vladimir Nabokov's 'Lolita'.

portmanteau word

an artificial word made up of parts of others, so called because of two meanings combined in one word.

post-aesthetic movement

an artistic response made by African Americans to the black aesthetic movement of the 1960s and early '70s. Writers since that time have adopted a somewhat different tone in their work, with less emphasis placed on the disparity between black and white in the United States. In the words of post-aesthetic authors such as Toni Morrison, John Edgar Wideman and Kristin Hunter, African Americans are portrayed as looking inward for answers to their own questions, rather than always looking to the outside world.

Two well-known examples of works produced as part of the post-aesthetic movement are the Pulitzer Prize-winning novels 'The Color Purple' by Alice Walker and 'Beloved' by Toni Morrison.

postcolonial criticism

an approach to literature that focuses on the study of cultural behaviour and expression in relationship to the colonised world. Postcolonial criticism refers to the analysis of literary works written by writers from countries and cultures that at one time have been controlled by colonising powers—such as Indian writers during or after British colonial rule. Postcolonial criticism also refers to the analysis of literary works written about colonial cultures by writers from the colonising country. Many of these kinds of analyses point out how writers from colonial powers sometimes misrepresent colonised cultures by reflecting more their own values.

postmodernism

writing from the 1960s forward characterised by experimentation and continuing to apply some of the fundamentals of modernism, which included existentialism and alienation. Postmodernists have gone a step further in the rejection of tradition begun with the modernists by also rejecting traditional forms, preferring the anti-novel over the novel and the anti-hero over the hero.

Postmodern writers include Alain Robbe-Grillet, Thomas Pynchon, Margaret Drabble, John Fowles, Adolfo Bioy-Casares and Gabriel Garcia Marquez.

Alain Robbe-Grillet

poulter's measure

a meter consisting of alternate Alexandrines and fourteeners, i.e., twelve-syllable and fourteen-syllable lines, a common measure in Elizabethan times.

■ **pre-Raphaelites**

a circle of writers and artists in mid nineteenth-century England. Valuing the pre-Renaissance artistic qualities of religious symbolism, lavish pictorialism and natural sensuousness, the Pre-Raphaelites cultivated a sense of mystery and melancholy that influenced later writers associated with the Symbolist and Decadent movements.

The major members of the group include Dante Gabriel Rossetti, Christina Rossetti, Algernon Swinburne and Walter Pater.

Walter Pater

■ **primitivism**

the belief that primitive peoples were nobler and less flawed than civilised peoples because they had not been subjected to the tainting influence of society.

Examples of literature espousing primitivism include Aphra Behn's 'Oroonoko: Or, The History of the Royal Slave', Jean-Jacques Rousseau's 'Julie ou la Nouvelle Heloise', Oliver Goldsmith's 'The Deserted Village', the poems of Robert Burns, Herman Melville's

Herman Melville

stories 'Typee, Omoo and Mardi', many poems of William Butler Yeats and Robert Frost and William Golding's novel 'Lord of the Flies'.

Robert Frost

■ **problem play**

popularised by Henrik Ibsen, a problem play is a type of drama that presents a social issue in order to awaken the audience to it. These plays usually reject romantic plots in favour of holding up a mirror that reflects not simply what the audience wants to see but what the playwright sees in them. Often, a problem play will propose a solution to the problem that does not coincide with prevailing opinion. The term is also used to refer to certain Shakespeare plays that do not fit the categories of tragedy, comedy, or romance.

■ **proceleusmatic**

a metrical foot consisting of four short syllables.

■ **procephalic**

in ancient prosody, having an excess of one syllable in the first foot of a line of verse.

■ **projective verse**

a form of free Verse in which the poet's breathing pattern determines the lines of the poem. Poets who advocate projective verse are against all formal structures in writing, including Meter and form.

Besides its creators, Robert Creeley, Robert Duncan and Charles Olson, two other well-known projective verse poets are Denise Levertov and LeRoi Jones (Amiri Baraka).

Also known as Breath Verse.

■ **prolepsis**

the application of an adjective to a noun in anticipation of the action of the verb.

■ **prologue**

an introductory section of a literary work. It often contains information establishing the situation of the characters and presents information about the setting, time period, or action. In drama, the prologue is spoken by a Chorus or by one of the principal characters.

In the 'General Prologue' of 'The Canterbury Tales', Geoffrey Chaucer describes the main characters and establishes the setting and purpose of the work.

■ **prose**

a literary medium that attempts to mirror the language of everyday speech. It is distinguished from poetry by its use of unmetered, unrhymed language consisting of logically related sentences. Prose is usually grouped into paragraphs that form a cohesive whole such as an essay or a novel.

Recognised masters of English prose writing include Sir Thomas Malory, William Caxton, Raphael Holinshed, Joseph Addison, Mark Twain and Ernest Hemingway.

■ **prose poem**

a genre in the poetic spectrum between free verse and prose. which is distinguishally poetic characteristics of rhythmic, aural and syntactic repetition, compression of thought, sustained intensity and patterned structure, but is set on the page in a continuous sequence of sentences as in prose, without line breaks.

■ **prosody**

the general term for the structure of poetry; the science of versification according to syllabic quantity, accent, etc.; the systematic study of poetic meter. All types of metrical feet, patterns of sound and rhyme, kinds of stanzaic forms, etc., fall within its domain.

prosopopeia

a figure of speech in which an imaginary or absent person is represented as speaking.

protagonist

the central character of a story who serves as a focus for its themes and incidents and as the principal rationale for its development. The protagonist is sometimes referred to in discussions of modern literature as the hero or anti-hero.

Well-known protagonists are Hamlet in William Shakespeare's 'Hamlet' and Jay Gatsby in F. Scott Fitzgerald's 'The Great Gatsby'.

protest fiction

protest fiction has as its primary purpose the protesting of some social injustice, such as racism or discrimination.

One example of protest fiction is a series of five novels by Chester Himes, beginning in 1945 with 'If He Hollers Let Him Go' and ending in 1955 with 'The Primitive'. These works depict the destructive effects of race and gender stereotyping in the context of interracial relationships. Another African American author whose works often revolve around themes of social protest is John Oliver Killens. James Baldwin's essay 'Everybody's Protest Novel' generated controversy by attacking the authors of protest fiction.

prothalamium or prothalamion

a song or poem in honour of a bride and bridegroom before their wedding.

proverb

a brief, sage saying that expresses a truth about life in a striking manner.

'They are not all cooks who carry long knives' is an example of a proverb.

pseudonym

a name assumed by a writer, most often intended to prevent his or her identification as the author of a work. Two or more authors may work together under one pseudonym, or an author may use a different name for each genre he or she publishes in. Some publishing companies maintain 'house pseudonyms' under which any number of authors may write installations in a series. Some authors also choose a pseudonym over their real names the way an actor may use a stage name. Examples of pseudonyms (with the author's real name in parentheses) include Voltaire (Francois-Marie Arouet), Novalis (Friedrich von

Hardenberg), Currer Bell (Charlotte Bronte), Ellis Bell (Emily Bronte), George Eliot (Maryann Evans), Honorio Bustos Donmecq (Adolfo Bioy-Casares and Jorge Luis Borges) and Richard Bachman (Stephen King).

George Elliot

■ psychological criticism

an approach to literature that draws upon psychoanalytic theories, especially those of Sigmund Freud or Jacques Lacan to understand more fully the text, the writer and the reader. The basis of this approach is the idea of the existence of a human unconscious—those impulses, desires and feelings about which a person is unaware but which influence emotions and behaviour. Critics use psychological approaches to explore the motivations of characters and the symbolic meanings of events, while biographers speculate about a writer's own motivations—conscious or unconscious—in a literary work. Psychological approaches are also used to describe and analyse the reader's personal responses to a text.

■ pun

a play on words that have similar sounds but different meanings.

A serious example of the pun is from John Donne's 'A Hymne to God the Father':

Sweare by thyself, that at my death thy sonne

Shall shine as he shines now and hereto fore;

And, having done that, Thou haste done;

I fear no more.

Shakespeare and other writers use puns extensively, for serious and comic purposes; in Romeo and Juliet (III.i.101), the dying Mercutio puns, 'Ask for me tomorrow and you shall find me a grave man'. Puns have serious literary uses, but since the eighteenth century, puns have been used almost purely for humorous effect.

■ pure poetry

poetry written without instructional intent or moral purpose that aims only to please a reader by its imagery or musical flow. The term pure poetry is used as the antonym of the term 'didacticism'.

The poetry of Edgar Allan Poe, Stephane Mallarme, Paul Verlaine, Paul Valery, Juan Ramoz Jimenez and Jorge Guillen offer examples of pure poetry.

■ pyramidal pattern

see **plot.**

pyrrhic

common in classic Greek poetry, a metrical foot consisting of two short or unaccented syllables, as in the third foot of: The slings | and ar | rows of | outra | geous for | tune

quantitative meter

a metrical system based on the length or 'weight' of syllables, rather than on stress. This is the norm in classical Latin and Greek, but is rare in English. Sir Philip Sidney (1554-86) made some attempts to write in quantitative meter in order to bring English poetry closer to its classical models, but he had few imitators.

quantitive verse

verse, which, rather than on the syllabic count or accent, is based on a systematic succession of long and short syllables, i.e., syllables which take a longer or shorter quantity of time to pronounce. When the lines are properly read, with the speed of articulation determined by varying vowel length and consonant groupings, the rhythmic pattern develops naturally. The unit of measure in quantitive verse is the mora.

quatorzain

a sonnet or any poem of fourteen lines.

quatrain

a four-line stanza of a poem or an entire poem consisting of four lines.

The following quatrain is from Robert Herrick's 'To Live Merrily and to Trust to Good Verses': Round, round, the root do's run; And being ravisht thus, Come, I will drink a Tun To my Propertius.

Robert Herrick

Queen's English

see **King's English.**

quintet or quintain

a poem, unit or stanza of five lines of verse.

R.K. Narayan (1906-2001)

Rasipuram Krishnaswamy Narayan was a highly celebrated Indian author. He was born in Madras (now Chennai). His first novel, *Swami and Friends* (1935), was based on his experiences as a village schoolteacher. Like his later fiction *The English Teacher* (1945) and *The Vendor of Sweets* (1967), it is a gently humorous, elegantly crafted picture of daily life in a fictitious southern Indian town. Narayan's other novels include *Waiting for the Mahatma* (1955), *The Guide* (1958), *The Man-Eater of*

Malgudi (1961) and *A Tiger for Malgudi* (1983).

A Horse and Two Goats (1970), *Malgudi Days* (1982) and *Grandmother's Tale* (1994) are collections of Narayan's short stories and contain simple, yet insightful, character portrayals that often reveal subtle ironies. He also revived the classic Indian epics *The Ramayana* (1972) and *The Mahabharata* (1978), condensing the lengthy works and setting them in modern surroundings.

■ Rabindranath Tagore (1861-1941)

Rabindranath Tagore was a renowned Indian poet, philosopher and Nobel laureate, who tried to intensify mutual Indian and Western cultural understanding. He was born in Calcutta (now Kolkata), into a wealthy family. He began to write poetry as a child. His first book appeared when he was 17 years old. After a brief stay in England (1878) to study law, he returned to India, where he rapidly became the most important and popular author of the colonial era, writing poetry, short stories, novels and plays. He composed several hundred popular songs and in 1929 also began painting.

A dedicated internationalist and educator, Tagore established a school (1901) in his estate, Santiniketan, in Bengal, to teach a blend of Eastern and Western philosophies. Tagore wrote primarily in Bengali, but translated many of his works into English himself. He was awarded the 1913 Nobel Prize in literature and in 1915 he was knighted by the British king George V. Tagore renounced his knighthood in 1919 following the Amritsar massacre of nearly 400 Indian demonstrators by British troops.

■ raisonneur

a character in a drama who functions as a spokesperson for the dramatist's views. The raisonneur typically observes the play without becoming central to its action.

Raisonneurs were very common in plays of the nineteenth century.

■ Ralph Waldo Emerson (1803-1882)

Ralph Waldo Emerson, American poet and essayist. His essays, poems and lectures made him a major figure in American literature. In the early 1830s he started his career as a writer and lecturer. He published his essay Nature in 1836. He attracted wide attention with *The American Scholar*, his Phi Beta Kappa oration at Harvard in 1837. Emerson joined *The Dial* in 1840. The first collection of Emerson's poems appeared in 1847. Among his best-known poems are *Threnody, Brahma, The Problem, The Rhodora* and *The Concord Hymn.* Emerson became famous with his winter lectures and they were published finally in a series of Essays in 1841 and the next series came out in 1844. The most notable among them are *The Over-Soul, Compensation* and *Self-Reliance*. From 1845–47 he delivered a series of lectures published as *Representative Men* (1850). His later lecture tours are contained in *The Conduct of Life* (1860) and *Society and Solitude* (1870). No writer has so profoundly influenced American thought as Emerson.

■ reader-response criticism

an approach to literature that focuses on the reader rather than the work itself, by attempting to describe what goes on in the reader's mind during the reading of a text. Hence, the consciousness of the reader-produced by reading the work-is the actual subject of reader-response criticism. These critics are not after a 'correct' reading of the text or what the author presumably intended; instead, they are interested in the reader's individual experience with the text. Thus, there is no single definitive reading of a work, because readers create rather than discover absolute meanings in texts. However, this approach is not a rationale for mistaken or bizarre readings, but an exploration of the possibilities for a plurality of readings. This kind of strategy calls attention to how we read and what influences our readings and what that reveals about ourselves.

■ realism

a nineteenth-century European literary movement that sought to portray familiar characters, situations and settings in a realistic manner. This was done primarily by using an objective narrative point of view and through the build-up of accurate detail. The standard for success of any realistic work depends on how faithfully it transfers common experience into fictional forms. The realistic method may be altered or extended, as in stream of consciousness writing, to record highly subjective experience.

Seminal authors in the tradition of realism include Honore de Balzac, Gustave Flaubert and Henry James.

Gustave Flaubert

■ recognition

the moment in a story when previously unknown or withheld information is revealed to the protagonist, resulting in the discovery of the truth of his or her situation and, usually, a decisive change in course for that character. In Oedipus the King, the moment of recognition comes when Oedipus finally realises that he has killed his father and married his mother.

reduplicated words

see **ricochet words.**

refrain

a phrase repeated at intervals throughout a poem. A refrain may appear at the end of each stanza or at less regular intervals. It may be altered slightly at each appearance.

Some refrains are nonsense expressions — as with 'Nevermore' in Edgar Allan Poe's 'The Raven' — that seem to take on a different significance with each use.

register

a term designating the appropriateness of a given style to a given situation. Speakers and writers in specific situations deploy, for example, a technical vocabulary (e.g. scientific, commercial, medical, legal, theological, psychological), as well as other aspects of style customarily used in that situation. Literary effect is often created by switching register.

Renaissance

the period in European history that marked the end of the Middle Ages. It began in Italy in the late fourteenth century. In broad terms, it is usually seen as spanning the fourteenth, fifteenth and sixteenth centuries, although it did not reach Great Britain, for example, until the 1580s or so. The Renaissance saw an awakening in almost every sphere of human activity, especially science, philosophy and the arts. The period is best defined by the emergence of a general philosophy that emphasised the importance of the intellect, the individual and world affairs. It contrasts strongly with the medieval worldview, characterised by the dominant concerns of faith, the social collective and spiritual salvation.

Prominent writers during the Renaissance include Niccolo Machiavelli and Baldassare

Niccolo Machiavelli

Castiglione in Italy, Miguel de Cervantes and Lope de Vega in Spain, Jean Froissart and Francois Rabelais in France, Sir Thomas More and Sir Philip Sidney in England and Desiderius Erasmus in Holland.

Francois Rabelais

repartee

conversation featuring snappy retorts and witticisms.

Masters of repartee include Sydney Smith, Charles Lamb and Oscar Wilde. An example is recorded in the meeting of 'Beau' Nash and John Wesley: Nash said, 'I never make way for a fool' to which Wesley responded, 'Don't you? I always do' and stepped aside.

repetend

the irregular repetition of a word, phrase, or line in a poem. It is a type of refrain, but differs in that it can appear at various places in the poem and may be only a partial repetition.

repetition

a basic artistic device, fundamental to any conception of poetry. It is a highly effective unifying force; the repetition of sound, syllables, words, syntactic elements, lines, stanzaic forms and metrical patterns establishes cycles of expectation which are reinforced with each successive fulfilment.

resolution

the portion of a story following the climax, in which the conflict is resolved.

The resolution of Jane Austen's 'Northanger Abbey' is neatly summed up in the following sentence: 'Henry and Catherine were married, the bells rang and every body smiled'.

resonance

the quality of richness or variety of sounds in poetic texture.

responsion

when stanzas are of the same meter, the same rhyme scheme and same number of lines they are 'in responsion'

restoration

see **restoration age.**

restoration age

a period in English literature beginning with the crowning of Charles II in 1660 and running to about 1700. The era, which was characterised by a reaction against Puritanism, was the first great age of the comedy of manners. The finest literature of the era is typically witty and urbane.

Prominent Restoration Age writers include William Congreve, Samuel Pepys, John Dryden and John Milton.

Samuel Pepys

■ **revenge tragedy**

a dramatic form popular during the Elizabethan Age, in which the protagonist, directed by the ghost of his murdered father or son, inflicts retaliation upon a powerful villain. Notable features of the revenge tragedy include violence, bizarre criminal acts, intrigue, insanity, a hesitant protagonist and the use of soliloquy.

Thomas Kyd's 'Spanish Tragedy' is the first example of revenge tragedy in English and William Shakespeare's 'Hamlet' is perhaps the best. Extreme examples of revenge tragedy, such as John Webster's 'The Duchess of Malfi', are labelled 'tragedies of blood'.

■ **reversal**

the point in a story when the protagonist's fortunes turn in an unexpected direction.

■ **revista**

the Spanish term for a vaudeville musical revue.

Examples of revistas include Antonio Guzman Aguilera's 'Mexico para los mexicanos', Daniel Vanegas's 'Maldito jazz' and Don Catarino's 'Whiskey, morfina y marihuana' and 'El desterrado'.

■ **rhapsody**

the recitation of a short epic poem or a longer epic abridged for recitation.

■ **rhetoric**

in literary criticism, this term denotes the art of ethical persuasion. In its strictest sense, rhetoric adheres to various principles developed since classical times for arranging facts and ideas in a clear, persuasive, appealing manner. The term is also used to refer to effective prose in general and theories of or methods for composing effective prose.

Classical examples of rhetorics include 'The Rhetoric of Aristotle', Quintillian's 'Institutio Oratoria' and Cicero's 'Ad Herennium'.

Aristotle

■ **rhetorical question**

a question intended to provoke thought, but not an expressed answer, in the reader. It is most commonly used in oratory and other persuasive genres.

The following lines from Thomas Gray's 'Elegy Written in a Country Churchyard' ask rhetorical questions:

Can storied urn or animated bust
Back to its mansion call the fleeting breath?
Can Honour's voice provoke the silent dust,

Or Flattery soothe the dull cold ear of Death?

■ rhopalic

having each succeeding unit in a poetic structure longer than the preceding one. Applied to a line, it means that each successive word is a syllable longer that its predecessor. Applied to a stanza, each successive line is longer by either a syllable or a metrical foot. Rhopalic verse is also called wedge verse.

■ rhyme

when used as a noun in literary criticism, this term generally refers to a poem in which words sound identical or very similar and appear in parallel positions in two or more lines. Rhymes are classified into different types according to where they fall in a line or stanza or according to the degree of similarity they exhibit in their spellings and sounds. Some major types of rhyme are 'masculine' rhyme, 'feminine' rhyme and 'triple' rhyme. In a masculine rhyme, the rhyming sound falls in a single accented syllable, as with 'heat' and 'eat'. Feminine rhyme is a rhyme of two syllables, one stressed and one unstressed, as with 'merry' and 'tarry'. Triple rhyme matches the sound of the accented syllable and the two unaccented syllables that follow: 'narrative' and 'declarative'.

Robert Browning alternates feminine and masculine rhymes in his 'Soliloquy of the Spanish Cloister':

Gr-r-r — there go, my heart's abhorrence!
Water your damned flower-pots, do!
If hate killed men, Brother Lawrence, God's blood, would not mine kill you!

Robert Browning

What? Your myrtle-bush wants trimming?
Oh, that rose has prior claims —
Needs its leaden vase filled brimming?
Hell dry you up with flames!

Thomas Hood

Triple rhymes can be found in Thomas Hood's 'Bridge of Sighs', George Gordon Byron's satirical verse and Ogden Nash's comic poems.

■ **rhyme royal**

a stanza of seven lines composed in iambic pentameter and rhymed ababbcc. The name is said to be a tribute to King James I of Scotland, who made much use of the form in his Poetry.

Examples of rhyme royal include Geoffrey Chaucer's 'The Parlement of Foules', William Shakespeare's 'The Rape of Lucrece', William Morris's 'The Early Paradise' and John Masefield's 'The Widow in the Bye Street'.

John Masefield

■ **rhyme scheme**

see **rhyme.**

■ **rhyme scheme**

the pattern established by the arrangement of rhymes in a stanza or poem, generally described by using letters of the alphabet to denote the recurrence of rhyming lines, such as the ababbcc of the Rhyme Royal stanza form.

■ **rhyming slang**

a slang popular in Great Britain in the early part of the 20th century, in which a word was replaced by a word or phrase that rhymed with it, as 'loaf of bread' for 'head'. When the rhyme was a compound word or part of a phrase, the rhyming part was often dropped, so in the foregoing example, 'loaf' would come to stand for 'head'.

■ **rhythm**

a regular pattern of sound, time intervals, or events occurring in writing, most often and most discernably in Poetry. Regular, reliable rhythm is known to be soothing to humans, while interrupted, unpredictable, or rapidly changing rhythm is disturbing. These effects are known to authors, who use them to produce a desired reaction in the reader.

■ **rich rhyme**

see **perfect rhyme.**

■ **ricochet words**

hyphenated words, usually formed by reduplicating a word with a change in the radical vowel or the initial consonant sound, such as 'pitter-patter', 'chit-chat', 'riff-raff', 'wishy-washy', 'hob-nob', 'roly-poly', 'pell-mell', 'razzle-dazzle', etc.

■ **riding rhyme**

an early form of heroic verse, so named for its use by Chaucer to describe the riding of the pilgrims in 'The Canterbury Tales'.

rising action

the part of a drama where the plot becomes increasingly complicated. Rising action leads up to the climax, or turning point, of a drama.

The final 'chase scene' of an action film is generally the rising action, which culminates in the film's climax.

rising meter

see **meter.**

Robert Browning (1812-1889)

Robert Browning, an English poet. In 1833, his first poem, Pauline, was published anonymously. *Paracelsus* (1835) and *Sordello* (1840) bought him recognition. In 1837, Browning began writing for the stage. He was not very successful but he still wrote eight verse plays during the next nine years. In 1841 the narrative poem *Pippa Passes* was published. This poem and subsequent poems were later published collectively as *Bells and Pomegranates* (1846) some of the poems included were *My Last Duchess* and *Soliloquy of the Spanish Cloister* both dramatic monologues. He proved his poetic genius with this medium. Other notable poems of this kind are *Fra Lippo Lippi andrea del Sarto* and *The Bishop Orders His Tomb.* While living in Italy he wrote *Christmas Eve* and *Easter Day* (1850) and *Men and Women* (1855). On his return to England he wrote *Dramatis Personae* (1864). This was followed by the murder story *The Ring and the Book* that was considered as his masterpiece. Societies were instituted for the study of his work in England and America. His later works include *Dramatic Idyls* (1879–80) and *Asolando* (1889). He was an important influence on the 20th-century poetry. He was buried in Westminster Abbey.

Robert Frost (1874-1963)

Robert Frost is regarded as the most popular and beloved American poet of the 20th-century. Frost wrote of the character, people and landscape of New England. In 1912 he went to England and received his first acclaim as a poet. He returned to United States after the publication of *A Boy's Will* (1913) and *North of Boston* (1914). He made several goodwill trips for the U.S. State Department .He recited his poem *The Gift Outright* at the inauguration of President John F. Kennedy in 1961. Among Frost's volumes of poetry are *New Hampshire* (1923), *West-running Brook* (1928), *Collected Poems* (1930), *A Further Range* (1936), *A Witness Tree* (1942), *Steeple Bush* (1947) and *In the Clearing* (1962). His blank verse plays were *A Masque of Reason* (1945) and *A Masque of Mercy* (1947). He was much more then a regional poet, his poems often had deep symbolic, even metaphysical, significance. His poems are concerned with human tragedies and fears, his reaction to the complexities of life and his ultimate acceptance of his burdens. Frost was awarded the Pulitzer Prize for poetry in 1924, 1931, 1937 and 1943.

■ rococo

a style of European architecture that flourished in the eighteenth century, especially in France. The most notable features of rococo are its extensive use of ornamentation and its themes of lightness, gaiety and intimacy. In literary criticism, the term is often used disparagingly to refer to a decadent or over-ornamental style.

Alexander Pope's 'The Rape of the Lock' is an example of literary rococo.

■ roman a clef

a French phrase meaning 'novel with a key'. It refers to a narrative in which real persons are portrayed under fictitious names.

Jack Kerouac, for example, portrayed various real-life beat generation figures under fictitious names in his 'On the Road'.

■ romance

a broad term, usually denoting a narrative with exotic, exaggerated, often idealised characters, scenes and themes.

Nathaniel Hawthorne called his 'The House of the Seven Gables' and 'The Marble Faun' romances in order to distinguish them from clearly realistic works.

■ romantic age

see **romanticism.**

■ romanticism

this term has two widely accepted meanings. In historical criticism, it refers to a European intellectual and artistic movement of the late eighteenth and early nineteenth centuries that sought greater freedom of personal expression than that allowed by the strict rules of literary form and logic of the eighteenth-century neo-classicists. The Romantics preferred emotional and imaginative expression to rational analysis. They considered the individual to be at the centre of all experience and so placed him or her at the centre of their art. The Romantics believed that the creative imagination reveals nobler truths — unique feelings and attitudes — than those that could be discovered by logic or by scientific examination. Both the natural world and the state of childhood were important sources for revelations of 'eternal truths'. 'Romanticism' is also used as a general term to refer to a type of sensibility found in all periods of literary history and usually considered to be in opposition to the principles of classicism. In this sense, Romanticism signifies any work or philosophy in which the exotic or dreamlike figure strongly, or that is devoted to individualistic expression, self-analysis, or a pursuit of a higher realm of knowledge than can be discovered by human reason.

Prominent Romantics include Jean-Jacques Rousseau, William Wordsworth, John Keats, Lord Byron and Johann Wolfgang von Goethe.

■ **romantics**

see **romanticism.**

■ **rondeau**

a fixed form used mostly in light or witty verse, usually consisting of fifteen octo or decasyllabic lines in three stanzas, with only two rhymes used throughout. A word or words from the first part of the first line are used as a (usually unrhymed) refrain ending the second and third stanzas, so the rhyme scheme is aabba aabR aabbaR.

■ **rondel**

a variation of the rondeau in which the first two lines of the first stanza are repeated as the last two lines of the second and third stanzas, thus a rhyme scheme of ABba abAB abbaA(B). (Sometimes only the first line of the poem is repeated at the end.)

■ **rondelet**

a short variation of the rondeau consisting generally of one 7-line stanza with two rhymes. The first line has four syllables and is repeated as a refrain forming the third and seventh lines; the other lines have eight syllables each.

■ **round character**

see **character.**

■ **roundel**

a variation of the rondeau devised by A. C. Swinburne, demonstrated in his poem, 'The Roundel'. He shortened the stanzas and moved the first refrain from the second to the first stanza, thus revising the rhyme scheme to abaR bab abaR.

A. C. Swinburne

■ **roundelay**

a poem with a refrain repeated frequently or at fixed intervals, as in a rondel.

■ **rune**

a Finnish or Old Norse poem.

■ **run-on couplet**

see **open couplet.**

■ **run-on lines**

lines in which the thought continues into the next line, as opposed to end-stopped.

■ **Russian symbolism**

a Russian poetic movement, derived from French symbolism, that flourished between 1894 and 1910. While some Russian

Symbolists continued in the French tradition, stressing aestheticism and the importance of suggestion above didactic intent, others saw their craft as a form of mystical worship and themselves as mediators between the supernatural and the mundane.

Russian symbolists include Aleksandr Blok, Vyacheslav Ivanovich Ivanov, Fyodor Sologub andrey Bely, Nikolay Gumilyov and Vladimir Sergeyevich Solovyov.

Sergeyevich Solovyov.

■ Salman Rushdie (1947–)

Salman Rushdie is a British novelist. He was born in Bombay. His first novels, including *Midnight's Children* (1981) and *Shame* (1983), are examples of magic realism, elements of this technique can also be found in his later fiction. Parts of his allegorical novel *Satanic Verses* (1988) were deemed sacrilegious and enraged many Muslims, including the Ayatollah Khomeini, who in 1989 issued a fatwa sentencing Rushdie to death. Violence occurred in cities where the book was sold and Rushdie went into hiding. From his seclusion he wrote *Haroun and the Sea of Stories* (1990), a novelistic allegory against censorship, East, West (1995), a book of short stories and *The Moor's Last Sigh* (1995), a novel that examines India's recent history through the life of a Jewish-Christian family. The fatwa was lifted in 1998. Rushdie's next novel, *The Ground beneath Her Feet* (1999), mingles myth and reality in a surreal world of rock-and-roll celebrity. He has also written a later novel, *Fury* (2001) and numerous essays.

■ Samuel Butler (1835–1902)

Samuel Butler was an English author. He was the son and grandson of eminent clergymen. Besides exhibiting some of his paintings (1868–76) at the Royal Academy, he composed several works in collaboration with Henry Festings Jones, among them the *Handelian Narcissus: A Dramatic Cantata* (1888). His *Erewhon*, in which he satirised English social and economic injustices by describing a country in which manners and laws were the reverse of those in England, appeared in 1872. It brought Butler immediate literary fame. In 1901, *Erewhon Revisited* was published. Butler opposed Darwin's explanation of evolution, finding it too mechanistic and he expounded his own theories in *Evolution Old and New* (1879), *Unconscious Memory* (1880) and *Luck or Cunning as the Main Means of Organic Modification?* (1887). In his single novel, the autobiographical *The Way of All Flesh* (1903), he attacked the Victorian pattern of life, in particular the ecclesiastical environment in which he was reared. Brilliantly ironic and witty, The Way of All Flesh is ranked among the great English novels. In 1912, Butler's notebooks were published.

Samuel Taylor Coleridge (1772–1834)

Coleridge, an English poet and a man of letters, was born in Ottery St. Mary, Devonshire. He is acknowledged as one of the most brilliant, versatile and influential figures in the English Romantic Movement. In 1794 he met the poet Robert Southey, who shared his political and social idealism. In 1795 Coleridge married Sarah Fricker, with whom he was never happy. They settled in Nether Stowey in 1797 and shortly thereafter William Wordsworth and his sister Dorothy moved into a house nearby.

It was not until his friendship with Wordsworth that he wrote his best poems. In 1798 Coleridge and Wordsworth jointly published the volume *Lyrical Ballads*. Coleridge's main contribution to the volume was the haunting, dreamlike ballad *The Rime of the Ancient Mariner*. This long poem, as well as *Kubla Khan* and *Christabel*, are his best-known works. *Dejection: An Ode*, published in 1802, was the last of Coleridge's great poems.

He continued his studies and writings on philosophy, religion, contemporary affairs and literature. In 1808 he separated from his wife permanently and from 1816 until his death he lived in London at the home of Dr. James Gilman, who brought his opium habit under control.

sapphic verse

after the odes of the Greek lyric poet, Sappho, a verse of eleven syllables in five feet, of which the first, fourth and fifth are trochees, the second a spondee and the third a dactyl. The Sapphic strophe consists of three Sapphic verses followed by an Adonic.

sarcasm

see **irony.**

satire

a work that uses ridicule, humour and wit to criticise and provoke change in human nature and institutions. There are two major types of satire: 'formal' or 'direct' satire speaks directly to the reader or to a character in the work; 'indirect' satire relies upon the ridiculous behaviour of its characters to make its point. Formal satire is further divided into two manners: the 'Horatian' which ridicules gently and the 'Juvenalian' which derides its subjects harshly and bitterly.

Voltaire's novella 'Candide' is an indirect satire. Jonathan Swift's essay 'A Modest Proposal' is a Juvenalian satire.

■ **scan**

to mark off lines of poetry into rhythmic units, or feet, to provide a visual representation of their metrical structure.

■ **scansion**

the analysis or 'scanning' of a poem to determine its Meter and often its rhyme scheme. The most common system of scansion uses accents (slanted lines drawn above syllables) to show stressed syllables, breves (curved lines drawn above syllables) to show unstressed syllables and vertical lines to separate each Foot.

In the first line of John Keats's 'Endymion',

'A thing of beauty is a joy forever:'

the word 'thing' the first syllable of 'beauty' the word 'joy' and the second syllable of 'forever' are stressed, while the words 'A' and 'of' the second syllable of 'beauty' the word 'a' and the first and third syllables of 'forever' are unstressed. In the second line:

'Its loveliness increases; it will never'

a pair of vertical lines separate the foot ending with 'increases' and the one beginning with 'it'.

■ **scene**

a subdivision of an Act of a drama, consisting of continuous action taking place at a single time and in a single location. The beginnings and endings of scenes may be indicated by clearing the stage of actors and props or by the entrances and exits of important characters.

The first act of William Shakespeare's 'Winter's Tale' is comprised of two scenes.

■ **science fiction**

a type of narrative about or based upon real or imagined scientific theories and technology. Science fiction is often peopled with alien creatures and set on other planets or in different dimensions.

Karel Capek's 'R.U.R'. is a major work of science fiction.

■ **scop**

an Old English poet or a poet troubadour of early Teutonic poetry.

■ **script**

the written text of a play, which includes the dialogue between characters, stage directions and often other expository information. See also **drama, exposition, prologue, stage directions**.

■ **Seamus Heaney (1939)**

Seamus Heaney, Irish poet, regarded as finest poet writing in English today. His early works include *Death of a Naturalist* (1966) and *Door into the Dark* (1969). In works such as *North* (1975), *Field Work* (1979) and *The Haw Lantern* (1987), Heaney attempts to grapple with Ireland's bloody past and troubled present. *In Station Island* (1984), he tries to come to terms with his own exile. Later poems, alternately elegiac and visionary, are included in *Seeing Things* (1991), *The Spirit Level* (1996) and *Electric Light* (2001). Heaney's carefully crafted poetry has been praised for its powerful imagery, meaningful content, musical phrasing and compelling rhythms. He was awarded Nobel Prize for Literature in 1995. Many of his critical and autobiographical essays were collected in *Preoccupations* (1980) and *The Government of the Tongue* (1989). His works in this genre including the medieval *Irish Sweeney Astray* (1984), *Sophocles's Philoctetes*, the highly acclaimed Beowulf and *the Libretto of Jan´cek's song cycle Diary of One Who Vanished* (2001).

■ second person

see **point of view.**

■ semiotics

the study of how literary forms and conventions affect the meaning of language.

Semioticians include Ferdinand de Saussure, Charles Sanders Pierce, Claude Levi-Strauss, Jacques Lacan, Michel Foucault, Jacques Derrida, Roland Barthes and Julia Kristeva.

■ senryu

a three-line unrhymed Japanese poetic form structurally similar to the haiku, but dealing with human rather than physical nature, usually in an ironic or satiric vein.

■ sense pause

see **caesura.**

■ sentimentality

a pejorative term used to describe the effort by an author to induce emotional responses in the reader that exceed what the situation warrants.

■ septenarius

a verse consisting of seven feet.

■ septet

a stanza of seven lines.

■ serenade

a lover's song or poem of the evening.

■ serpentine verses

verses ending with the same word with which they begin.

■ sestet

a stanza of six lines, especially the last six lines of an Italian or Petrarchan sonnet.

■ sestet

a stanza consisting of exactly six lines.

■ sestina

a type of fixed form of poetry consisting of thirty-six lines of any length divided into six sestets and a three-line concluding stanza called an envoy. The six words at the end of the first sestet's lines must also appear at the ends of the other five sestets, in varying order. These six words must also appear in the envoy, where they often resonate important themes. An example of this highly demanding form of poetry is Elizabeth Bishop's 'Sestina'.

Elizabeth Bishop

■ **setting**

the time, place and culture in which the action of a narrative takes place. The elements of setting may include geographic location, characters' physical and mental environments, prevailing cultural attitudes, or the historical time in which the action takes place.
Examples of settings include the romanticised Scotland in Sir Walter Scott's 'Waverley' novels, the French provincial setting in Gustave Flaubert's 'Madame Bovary', the fictional Wessex country of Thomas Hardy's novels and the small towns of southern Ontario in Alice Munro's short stories.

Sir Walter Scott

■ **shakespearean sonnet**

see **sonnet.**

■ **shaped verse**

see **pattern poetry.**

■ **short fiction**

prose storytelling whose incidents are deeply revealing of human values. No length limits have ever been settled on. Usually, the reader's sense of satisfaction signals the completion of a story, but some of the stories purposely deny you a sense of satisfaction in order to bring you to a point of reflection and questioning

■ **short story**

a fictional prose narrative shorter and more focused than a novella. The short story usually deals with a single episode and often a single character. The 'tone' the author's attitude toward his or her subject and audience, is uniform throughout. The short story frequently also lacks denouement, ending instead at its climax.
Well-known short stories include Ernest Hemingway's 'Hills Like White Elephants' Katherine Mansfield's 'The Fly' Jorge Luis Borge's 'Tlon, Uqbar, Orbis Tertius' Eudora Welty's 'Death of a Travelling Salesman' Yukio Mishima's 'Three Million Men' and Milan Kundera's 'The Hitchhiking Game'.

■ **showing**

see **character.**

sight rhyme

words which are similar in spelling but different in pronunciation, like 'mow' and 'how' or 'height' and 'weight'. Some words that are sight rhymes today did have a correspondence of sound in earlier stages of the language.

sigmatism

the intentional repetition of words with sibilant speech sounds closely spaced in a line of poetry, as in,

She sells sea-shells by the sea shore

sign

a symbol in its aspect as a verbal representative of a natural object or concept.

signifying monkey

a popular trickster figure in black folklore, with hundreds of tales about this character documented since the 19th century.

Henry Louis Gates Jr. examines the history of the signifying monkey in 'The Signifying Monkey: Towards a Theory of Afro-American Literary Criticism', published in 1988.

sijo

a short Korean poetic form consisting of three lines, each line having a total of 14-16 syllables in four groups ranging from 2 to 7 (but usually 3 or 4) syllables, with a natural pause at the end of the second group and a major pause after the fourth group. The third line often introduces a resolution, a touch of humour, or a turn of thought. Though there are no restrictions on the subject matter, favoured ones include nature, virtue and rural life. The unique texture of the sijo derives from the blend of sound, rhythm and meaning. Western sijos are sometimes divided at the pauses and presented in six lines.

simile

a common figure of speech that makes an explicit comparison between two things by using words such as like, as, than, appears and seems 'A sip of Mrs. Cook's coffee is like a punch in the stomach'. The effectiveness of this simile is created by the differences between the two things compared. There would be no simile if the comparison were stated this way 'Mrs. Cook's coffee is as strong as the cafeteria's coffee'. This is a literal translation because Mrs. Cook's coffee is compared with something like it-another kind of coffee.

Sir Thomas Browne (1605–82)

Thomas Browne an English author, essayist and physician was born in London, educated at Oxford and abroad, knighted (1671) by Charles II. His *Religio Medici*, in which Browne attempted to reconcile science and religion, was written about 1635. After circulating in manuscript, it was first published in a pirated edition (1642), an authorised edition followed (1643). Inspired by the discovery of funeral urns near Norwich, he wrote *Hydriotaphia: Urn Burial* (1658), a solemn reflection on death and immortality, in which he expressed a belief in the futility of things here on earth. Published with Urn Burial was the more optimistic *The Garden of Cyrus*, a work devoted to the mystic symbolism of the number five. Browne's philosophy is now primarily of historical interest. It is the quality of his faith and particularly, his mode of expression that make him one of the outstanding figures in the history of English literature. His other notable works are *Pseudodoxia Epidemica* (1646), commonly known as Vulgar Errors and *Christian Morals* (1716).

■ Sir Walter Scott (1771–1832)

Sir Walter Scott was a Scottish novelist and poet, born in Edinburgh. He is considered the father of both the regional and the historical novel. He was made sheriff-deputy of Selkirkshire in 1799. His first published works (1796) were translations of two German ballads by Bürger, followed by a translation (1799) of Goethe's Götz von Berlichingen. His first novel, *Waverley* (1814), was an immediate success. There followed the Waverley novels that reveal Scott's great storytelling gift and his talent for vivid characterisation, like *Guy Mannering* (1815), *The Black Dwarf* (1816), *Rob Roy* (1818), *The Heart of Midlothian* (1818) and *The Legend of Montrose* (1819).

Ivanhoe (1820), was Scott's first prose reconstruction of a time long past. His public acclaim grew and in 1820 Scott was made a baronet. In 1825 Scott was ruined financially. The next few years' work included *Woodstock* (1826), *A life of Napoleon* (1827), *Chronicles of the Canongate* (1827) and *Anne of Geierstein* (1829). Scott's health began to fail in 1830. The author died in 1832.

■ situational irony

see **irony.**

■ skald

an ancient Scandinavian poet or bard.

■ skeltonics

named for their inventor, John Skelton, short verses of irregular meter with two or three stresses, sometimes in falling and sometimes in rising rhythm and usually with rhymed couplets.

■ slang

a type of informal verbal communication that is generally unacceptable for formal writing. Slang words and phrases are often colourful exaggerations used to emphasise the speaker's point; they may also be shortened versions of an often-used word or phrase.

Examples of American slang from the 1990s include 'yuppie' (an acronym for Young Urban Professional), 'awesome' (for 'excellent'), wired (for 'nervous' or 'excited') and 'chill out' (for relax).

slant rhyme

see **near rhyme.**

slave narrative

autobiographical accounts of American slave life as told by escaped slaves. These works first appeared during the abolition movement of the 1830s through the 1850s.

Olaudah Equiano's 'The Interesting Narrative of Olaudah Equiano, or Gustavus Vassa', 'The African' and Harriet Ann Jacobs's 'Incidents in the Life of a Slave Girl' are examples of the slave narrative.

Olaudah Equiano

social realism

see **socialist realism.**

socialist realism

the Socialist Realism school of literary theory was proposed by Maxim Gorky and established as a dogma by the first Soviet Congress of Writers. It demanded adherence to a communist worldview in works of literature. Its doctrines required an objective viewpoint comprehensible to the working classes and themes of social struggle featuring strong proletarian heroes.

A successful work of socialist realism is Nikolay Ostrovsky's 'Kak zakalyalas stal (How the Steel Was Tempered)'.

Also known as Social Realism.

society verse

a short lyrical poem written in an urbane manner or crisp, animated and typically ironic light verse dealing with contemporaneous topics.

sociological criticism

an approach to literature that examines social groups, relationships and values as they are manifested in literature. Sociological approaches emphasise the nature and effect of the social forces that shape power relationships between groups or classes of people. Such readings treat literature as either a document reflecting social conditions or a product of those conditions. The former view brings into focus the social milieu; the latter emphasises the work. Two important forms of sociological criticism are Marxist and feminist approaches. See also **feminist criticism, Marxist criticism.**

solecism

an impropriety of speech; a violation of the established rules of syntax.

soliloquy

a dramatic convention by means of which a character, alone on stage, utters his or her thoughts aloud. Playwrights use soliloquies as a convenient way to inform the audience about a character's motivations and state of mind. Shakespeare's Hamlet delivers perhaps the best known of all soliloquies, which begins 'To be or not to be'.

sonnet

a fixed form of lyric poetry that consists of fourteen lines, usually written in iambic pentameter. There are two basic types of sonnets, the Italian and the English. The Italian sonnet, also known as the Petrarchan sonnet, is divided into an octave, which typically rhymes abbaabba and a sestet, which may have varying rhyme schemes. Common rhyme patterns in the sestet are cdecde, cdcdcd and cdccdc. Very often the octave presents a situation, attitude, or problem that the sestet comments upon or resolves, as in John Keats's 'On First Looking into Chapman's Homer'. The English sonnet, also known as the Shakespearean sonnet, is organised into three quatrains and a couplet, which typically rhyme abab cdcd efef gg. This rhyme scheme is more suited to English poetry because English has fewer rhyming words than Italian. English sonnets, because of their four-part organisation, also have more flexibility with respect to where thematic breaks can occur. Frequently, however, the most pronounced break or turn comes with the concluding couplet, as in Shakespeare's 'Shall I compare thee to a summer's day?'

sonneteer

a composer of sonnets; also, the term is sometimes applied to a minor or insignificant poet.

Sophocles (496 B.C.–406 B.C.)

Sophocles was a Greek tragic dramatist. He was a younger contemporary of Aeschylus and older contemporary of Euripides, born in Colonus, near Athens. A man of wealth, charm and genius, Sophocles was given posts of responsibility in peace and in war by the Athenians. He was a general and a priest. After his death he was worshipped as a hero. At the age of 16 he led the chorus in a paean on the victory of Salamis. He won his first dramatic triumph in 468, over Aeschylus, and thenceforth wrote copiously (he composed about 123 dramas), winning first place about 20 times and never falling lower than second. *Ajax* is perhaps the earliest tragedy, three actors are used but the form is handled imperfectly. In his other plays, whether with two or three actors, the dialogue is polished and smooth. The most famous of his tragedies is *Oedipus Rex* or *Oedipus Tyrannus* (c. 429). *Oedipus at Colonus* was written shortly before Sophocles' death and was produced in 401. The characters in

Sophocles are governed in their fate more by their own faults than by the actions of the gods as in the tragedies of Aeschylus.

■ sotadic or sotadean

see **palindrome.**

■ sound devices

resources used by writers of verse to convey and reinforce the meaning or experience of poetry through the skilful use of sound.

■ speaker

the voice used by an author to tell a story or speak a poem. The speaker is often a created identity and should not automatically be equated with the author's self.

■ spenserian stanza

a nine-line stanza having eight Verses in iambic pentameter, its ninth verse in iambic hexameter and the rhyme scheme ababbcbcc.

This stanza form was first used by Edmund Spenser in his allegorical poem 'The Faerie Queene'.

■ spondee

in Poetry Meter, a Foot consisting of two long or stressed syllables occurring together. This form is quite rare in English Verse and is usually composed of two monosyllabic words.

The first foot in the following line from Robert Burns's 'Green Grow the Rashes' is an example of a spondee: Green grow the rashes, O.

■ sprung rhyme

a poetic rhythm characterised by feet varying from one to four syllables which are equal in time length but different in the number of syllables. It has only one stress per foot, falling on the first syllable, or on the only syllable if there is but one, which produces the frequent juxtaposition of single accented syllables.

■ stage directions

a playwright's instructions in a play concerning tone of voice, action, entrances and exits, lighting, music, sound effects and so forth. Example: Exit, pursued by a bear. (W. Shakespeare 'The Winter's Tale' III, iii, 57)

■ stanza

a subdivision of a poem consisting of lines grouped together, often in recurring patterns of rhyme, line length and meter. Stanzas may also serve as units of thought in a poem much like paragraphs in prose.

Examples of stanza forms include the quatrain, terza rima, ottava rima, Spenserian and the so-called. In Memoriam stanza from Alfred, Lord Tennyson's poem by that title. The following is an example of the latter form: 'Love is and was my lord and king and in his presence I attend To hear the tidings of my friend, Which every hour his couriers bring'.

■ stanza forms

The names given to describe the number of lines in a stanzaic unit, such as: couplet (2), tercet (3), quatrain (4), quintet (5), sestet (6), septet (7) and octave (8), some stanzas follow a set rhyme scheme and meter in addition to the number of lines and are given specific names to describe them, such as, ballad meter, ottava rima, rhyme royal, terza rima and Spenserian stanza.

static character

usually a minor figure who remains unchanged throughout a work.

stave

a verse, stanza or a metrical portion of a poem.

Stephen Vincent Benét (1898-1943)

Stephen Vincent Benet, American poet and author, brother of William Rose Benet. He was a student at Yale and graduated in 1919. Benét published several volumes of verse after graduating from college. Some of the verses that were published include *A Ballad of William Sycamore* (1923) and several novels, of which *Jean Huguenot* (1923) and *The Spanish Bayonet* (1926). These verses were some of his best work. He became famous after publication of *John Brown's Body* in 1928. He wrote a long narrative poem of the *Civil War* and got a Pulitzer Prize for it in 1929. He also wrote short stories. His notable short story was *The Devil and Daniel Webster.* He was unable to finish the poem *Western Star* that was about the westward migration. It was a long narrative poem and got published in 1943. Stephen was given the Pulitzer Prize again in 1944.

stereotype

a stereotype was originally the name for a duplication made during the printing process; this led to its modern definition as a person or thing that is (or is assumed to be) the same as all others of its type.

Common stereotypical characters include the absent-minded professor, the nagging wife, the troublemaking teenager and the kind-hearted grandmother.

stich

a line or verse of poetry.

stichomythia or stichomythy

a dramatic dialogue of lively repartee in alternate verse lines. (When half-lines instead of whole lines are used for this technique, it is called hemistichomythia)

stock responses

predictable, conventional reactions to language, characters, symbols, or situations. The flag, motherhood, puppies, God and peace are common objects used to elicit stock responses from unsophisticated audiences.

stornello verses

verses which include the repetition of certain words in changing order and varied placement.

strain

a passage or piece of poetry; a flow of eloquence, style or spirit in expression.

stream of consciousness

a narrative technique for rendering the inward experience of a character. This technique is designed to give the impression of an ever-changing series of thoughts, emotions, images and memories in the spontaneous and seemingly illogical order that they occur in life.

The textbook example of stream of consciousness is the last section of James Joyce's 'Ulysses'.

stress

the relative force or prominence of word sounds or syllables in verse, i.e., the degree of accent.

strophe

in modern poetry, a stanza or rhythmic system of two or more lines arranged as a unit. In classical poetry, a strophe is the first division in the triadic structure of Pindaric verse, corresponding metrically to the antistrophe which follows it; also, the stanza preceding or alternating with the antistrophe in ancient lyric poetry.

structuralism

a twentieth-century movement in literary criticism that examines how literary texts arrive at their meanings, rather than the meanings themselves. There are two major types of structuralist analysis: one examines the way patterns of linguistic structures unify a specific text and emphasise certain elements of that text and the other interprets the way literary forms and conventions affect the meaning of language itself.

Prominent structuralists include Michel Foucault, Roman Jakobson and Roland Barthes.

structure

the form taken by a piece of literature. The structure may be made obvious for ease of understanding, as in non-fiction works, or may be obscured for artistic purposes, as in some Poetry or seemingly 'unstructured' prose.

Examples of common literary structures include the plot of a narrative, the acts and scenes of a drama and such poetic forms as the Shakespearean sonnet and the Pindaric ode.

sturm und drang

a German term meaning 'storm and stress'. It refers to a German literary movement of the 1770s and 1780s that reacted against the order and rationalism of the enlightenment, focusing instead on the intense experience of extraordinary individuals.

Highly romantic, works of this movement, such as Johann Wolfgang von Goethe's 'Gotz von Berlichingen', are typified by realism, rebelliousness and intense emotionalism.

style

the distinctive and unique manner in which a writer arranges words to achieve particular effects. Style essentially combines the idea to be expressed with the individuality of the author. These arrangements include individual word choices as well as matters such as the length of sentences, their structure, tone and use of irony.

■ **subject**

the person, event, or theme at the centre of a work of literature. A work may have one or more subjects of each type, with shorter works tending to have fewer and longer works tending to have more.

The subjects of James Baldwin's novel 'Go Tell It on the Mountain' include the themes of father-son relationships, religious conversion, black life and sexuality. The subjects of Anne Frank's 'Diary of a Young Girl' include Anne and her family members as well as World War II, the Holocaust and the themes of war, isolation, injustice and racism.

Anne Frank

■ **subjectivity**

writing that expresses the author's personal feelings about his subject and which may or may not include factual information about the subject.

Subjectivity is demonstrated in James Joyce's 'Portrait of the Artist as a Young Man', Samuel Butler's 'The Way of All Flesh' and Thomas Wolfe's 'Look Homeward, Angel'.

■ **subplot**

the secondary action of a story, complete and interesting in its own right, that reinforces or contrasts with the main plot. There may be more than one subplot and sometimes as many as three, four, or even more, running through a piece of fiction. Subplots are generally either analogous to the main plot, thereby enhancing our understanding of it, or extraneous to the main plot, to provide relief from it.

■ **surrealism**

a term introduced to criticism by Guillaume Apollinaire and later adopted by Andre Breton. It refers to a French literary and artistic movement founded in the 1920s. The Surrealists sought to express unconscious thoughts and feelings in their works. The best-known technique used for achieving this aim was Automatic Writing — transcriptions of spontaneous outpourings from the unconscious. The Surrealists proposed to unify the contrary levels of conscious and unconscious, dream and reality, objectivity and subjectivity into a new level of 'super-realism'. Surrealism can be found in the poetry of Paul Eluard, Pierre Reverdy and Louis Aragon, among others.

■ **suspense**

a literary device in which the author maintains the audience's attention through the build-up of events, the outcome of which will soon be revealed.

Suspense in William Shakespeare's 'Hamlet' is sustained throughout by the question of whether or not the Prince will achieve what he has been instructed to do and of what he intends to do.

syllabic verse

a type of verse distinguished primarily by the syllable count, i.e., the number of syllables in each line, rather than by the rhythmical arrangement of accents or time quantities.

syllable

the smallest unit of speech that normally occurs in isolation, or a distinct sound element within a word. This can consist of a vowel alone ('O') or a combination of a vowel and one or more consonants ('no', 'not'). Monosyllables contain only one syllable ('dog', 'big', 'shoe'); polysyllables contain more than one syllable. The word 'syllable' contains three syllables.

syllepsis

a type of zeugma in which a single word, usually a verb or adjective, agrees grammatically with two or more other words, but semantically with only one, thereby effecting a shift in sense with the other, as in 'colder than ice and a usurer's heart'.

syllogism

a method of presenting a logical argument. In its most basic form, the syllogism consists of a major premise, a minor premise and a conclusion.

An example of a syllogism is:

Major premise: When it snows, the streets get wet.

Minor premise: It is snowing.

Conclusion: The streets are wet.

symbol

a person, object, image, word, or event that evokes a range of additional meaning beyond and usually more abstract than its literal significance. Symbols are educational devices for evoking complex ideas without having to resort to painstaking explanations that would make a story more like an essay than an experience. Conventional symbols have meanings that are widely recognized by a society or culture. Some conventional symbols are the Christian cross, the Star of David, a swastika, or a nation's flag. Writers use conventional symbols to reinforce meanings. Kate Chopin, for example, emphasises the spring setting in 'The Story of an Hour' as a way of suggesting the renewed sense of life that Mrs. Mallard feels when she thinks herself free from her husband. A literary or contextual symbol can be a setting, character, action, object, name, or anything else in a work that maintains its literal significance while suggesting other meanings. Such symbols go beyond conventional symbols; they gain their symbolic meaning within the context of a specific story. For example, the white whale in Melville's 'Moby-Dick' takes on multiple symbolic meanings in the work, but these meanings do not automatically carry over into other stories about whales. The meanings suggested by Melville's whale are specific to that text; therefore, it becomes a contextual symbol.

■ symbolism

this term has two widely accepted meanings. In historical criticism, it denotes an early modernist literary movement initiated in France during the nineteenth century that reacted against the prevailing standards of realism. Writers in this movement aimed to evoke, indirectly and symbolically, an order of being beyond the material world of the five senses. Poetic expression of personal emotion figured strongly in the movement, typically by means of a private set of symbols uniquely identifiable with the individual poet. The principal aim of the Symbolists was to express in words the highly complex feelings that grew out of everyday contact with the world. In a broader sense, the term 'symbolism' refers to the use of one object to represent another.

Early members of the Symbolist movement included the French authors Charles Baudelaire and Arthur Rimbaud; William Butler Yeats, James Joyce and T. S. Eliot were influenced as the movement moved to Ireland, England and the United States. Examples of the concept of symbolism include a flag that stands for a nation or movement, or an empty cupboard used to suggest hopelessness, poverty and despair.

■ symbolist

see **symbolism.**

■ symbolist movement

see **symbolism.**

■ symploce

the repetition of a word or expression at the beginnings plus the repetition of a word or expression at the end of successive phrases, i.e, a combination of both anaphora and epistrophe.

■ synaeresis or syneresis

a type of elision in which two contiguous vowels within a word which are normally pronounced as two syllables, as in seest, are pronounced as one syllable instead.

■ synaloepha or synalepha

a type of elision in which a vowel at the end of one word is coalesced with one beginning the next word, as 'th' embattled plain'.

■ syncopation

in the quantitive verse of classical poetry, the suppression of one syllable in a metrical pattern, with its time value either replaced by a pause (like a musician's 'rest') or by the additional lengthening of an adjoining long syllable.

■ syncope

a type of elision in which a word is contracted by removing one or more letters or syllables from the middle, as 'ne'er' for 'never', or 'fo'c'sle' for 'forecastle'.

■ synecdoche

a figure of speech in which a part of something stands for the whole or the whole for a part, as 'wheels' for 'automobile' or 'society' for 'high society'.

■ synesthesia or synaesthesia

the perception or description of one kind of sense impression in words normally used to describe a different sense, like a 'sweet voice' or a 'velvety smile'. It can be very effective for creating vivid imagery.

■ synesthetic metaphor

a metaphor that suggests a similarity between experiences in different senses, as 'a gourmet of country music'.

■ synonym

one or two or more words that have the same or nearly identical meanings.

■ syntax

the ordering of words into meaningful verbal patterns such as phrases, clauses and sentences. Poets often manipulate syntax, changing conventional word order, to place certain emphasis on particular words. Emily Dickinson, for instance, writes about being surprised by a snake in her poem A narrow Fellow in the Grass 'His notice sudden is'. In addition to the alliterative hissing s-sounds here, Dickinson also effectively manipulates the line's syntax so that the verb is appears unexpectedly at the end, making the snake's hissing presence all the more 'sudden'.

■ T. S. Eliot (1888-1965)

T.S. Eliot, American-British poet and critic. He won the 1948 Nobel Prize in Literature. In 1927 he became a British subject. He was assistant editor of the *Egoist* (1917–19) and edited his own quarterly, *The Criterion* (1922–39). Eliot's early poetical works—*Prufrock and Other Observations* (1917), *Poems* (1920) and *The Waste Land* (1922)—express the anguish and barrenness of modern life. The *Waste Land* compelled immediate critical attention. Eliot was an extraordinarily influential critic. His outstanding critical works are contained in such volumes as *The Sacred Wood* (1920), *For Lancelot Andrewes* (1928), *Selected Essays, 1917–1932* (1932), *The Use of Poetry and the Use of Criticism* (1933), *Elizabethan Essays* (1934), *Essays Ancient and Modern* (1936) and *Notes towards a Definition of Culture* (1948). Eliot's plays attempt to revitalise verse drama and usually treat the same themes as in his poetry. They include *Murder in the Cathedral* (1935), dealing with the final hours of Thomas à Becket, *The Family Reunion* (1939), *The Cocktail Party* (1950), *The Confidential Clerk* (1954) and *The Elder Statesman* (1959). His complete poems and plays appeared in 1969, his letters in 1988 and his previously unpublished early poems (1909–17) in 1996.

■ **tactile imagery**

verbal description that invokes the sense of touch.

■ **tag**

a syllable of extra light stress at the end of a line, not counted in the meter. Also known as 'feminine ending'.

■ **tagalied**

see **aubade.**

■ **tail rhyme**

also called caudate rhyme, a verse form in which rhyming lines, usually a couplet or triplet, are followed by a tail, a line of shorter length with a different rhyme; in a tail-rhyme stanza, the tails rhyme with each other.

■ **tale**

a story told by a narrator with a simple plot and little character development. Tales are usually relatively short and often carry a simple message. Examples of tales can be found in the work of Rudyard Kipling, Somerset Maugham, Saki, Anton Chekhov, Guy de Maupassant and Armistead Maupin.

Armistead Maupin

■ **tall tale**

a humorous tale told in a straightforward, credible tone but relating absolutely impossible events or feats of the characters. Such tales were commonly told of frontier adventures during the settlement of the west in the United States. Tall tales have been spun around such legendary heroes as Mike Fink, Paul Bunyan, Davy Crockett, Johnny Appleseed and Captain Stormalong as well as the real-life William F. Cody and Annie Oakley. Literary use of tall tales can be found in Washington Irving's 'History of New York', Mark Twain's 'Life on the Mississippi' and in the German R. F. Raspe's Baron Munchausen's Narratives of His Marvellous Travels and Campaigns in Russia.

■ **tanka**

a genre of Japanese poetry similar to the haiku. A tanka consists of thirty-one syllables arranged in five lines. The lines contain five / seven / five / seven / seven syllables. Also known as the waka or uta, it originated in the 600s CE and it is regarded as the classic, ancient Japanese poetic form. It has had little influence on Western poetry, though Amy Lowell and Adelaide Crapsey have imitated it.

Amy Lowell

■ tautology

the unnecessary and excessive repetition of the same idea in different words in the same sentence, as 'The room was completely dark and had no illumination' or 'A breeze greeted the dusk and nightfall was heralded by a gentle wind'.

■ telestich

see **acrostic.**

■ Tennessee Williams (1911–83)

Tennessee Williams original name was Thomas Lanier Williams, an American dramatist, was born in Columbus. He graduated from State University of Iowa, in 1938. One of America's foremost playwrights, the author of more than 70 plays, he achieved his first successes with the productions of *The Glass Menagerie* (1945) and *A Streetcar Named Desire* (1947, Pulitzer Prize). In these plays, Williams explores the intense passions and frustrations of a disturbed and frequently brutal society. He is noted for his scenes of high dramatic tension and for brilliant dialogue. He is perhaps most successful in his portraits of the oversensitive and lonely Southern woman, such as *Blanche in Streetcar*, clutching at life, particularly at her memories of a grand past that no longer exists. His other plays include *Summer and Smoke* (1948), *The Rose Tattoo* (1950), *Camino Real* (1953), *Cat on a Hot Tin Roof* (1955, Pulitzer) and *Small Craft Warnings* (1972). Williams's one-act plays were collected in *27 Wagons Full of Cotton* (1946) and *The American Blues* (1948). He also wrote collections of short fiction like *One Arm and Other Stories* (1948) and *Hard Candy* (1954).

■ tension

the artistically satisfying equilibrium of opposing forces in a poem, usually referring to the use of language and imagery, but often applied to other elements, such as dramatic structure, rhythmic patterns and sometimes to the aesthetic value of the poem as a whole.

■ tercet

a three-line unit or stanza of poetry. It typically rhymes in an AAA or ABA pattern.

■ terminus a quo

the earliest possible date that a literary work could have been written, a potential starting point for dating a manuscript or text. Latin for 'boundary from that point'.

■ terminus ad quem

the latest possible date that a literary work could have been written, a potential ending point for dating a manuscript or text. Latin for 'boundary up to this point'.

■ terza rima

a three-line stanza form in Poetry in which the rhymes are made on the last word of each line in the following manner: the first and third lines of the first stanza, then the second line of the first stanza and the first and third lines of the second stanza and so on with the middle line of any stanza rhyming with the first and third lines of the following stanza.

An example of terza rima is Percy Bysshe Shelley's 'The Triumph of Love': As in that trance of wondrous thought I lay This was the tenour of my waking dream. Methought I sate beside a public way Thick strewn with summer dust and a great stream Of people there was hurrying to and fro Numerous as gnats upon the evening gleam,...

Percy Bysshe Shelley

■ tetralogy

1. in a general sense, a collection of four narratives that are contiguous and continuous in chronology. Just as three books that tell a continuous story constitute a trilogy, four books that tell a continuous narrative are a tetralogy.

2. a set of four plays that constitute a long historical cycle, written in approximately the same half of Shakespeare's career. Scholars refer to Shakespeare as writing a 'First Tetralogy' (containing Richard III and Henry VI, part 1, part 2 and part 3) and a 'Second Tetralogy' (containing Richard II, Henry IV, part I., Henry IV, part 2 and Henry V.) Contrast with sequel and trilogy.

■ tetrameter

a line consisting of four metrical feet.

■ textual criticism

a branch of literary criticism that seeks to establish the authoritative text of a literary work. Textual critics typically compare all known manuscripts or printings of a single work in order to assess the meanings of differences and revisions. This procedure allows them to arrive at a definitive version that (supposedly) corresponds to the author's original intention. Textual criticism was applied during the Renaissance to salvage the classical texts of Greece and Rome and modern works have been studied, for instance, to undo deliberate correction or censorship, as in the case of novels by Stephen Crane and Theodore Dreiser.

Stephen Crane

■ **textual varient**

a version of a text that has alterations in wording or structure, especially one with missing lines or extra lines added. In some cases, textual variants reflect the difference between an author's early version or rough draft of a work and a later version or polished final product. Difference in Shakespeare's plays might have come about in the difference between the foul papers (handwritten rough drafts) and the fair copy (the largely corrected versions sent to the printers). Variations in Chaucer's manuscripts of The Canterbury Tales might reflect an earlier, alternative scheme for structuring the work that Chaucer later abandoned in favour of a revised order for the various tales. Other textual variants in literary works are the product of scribal corruption or errata.

■ **texture**

the 'feel' of a poem that comes from the interweaving of technical elements, syntax, patterns of sound and meaning.

■ **theatre in the round**

a performance taking place on an arena stage.

■ **theater of cruelty**

term used to denote a group of theatrical techniques designed to eliminate the psychological and emotional distance between actors and audience. This concept, introduced in the 1930s in France, was intended to inspire a more intense theatrical experience than conventional theatre allowed. The 'cruelty' of this dramatic theory signified not sadism but heightened actor/audience involvement in the dramatic event. The theatre of cruelty was theorised by Antonin Artaud in his 'Le Theatre et son double' (The Theatre and Its Double) and also appears in the work of Jerzy Grotowski, Jean Genet, Jean Vilar and Arthur Adamov, among others.

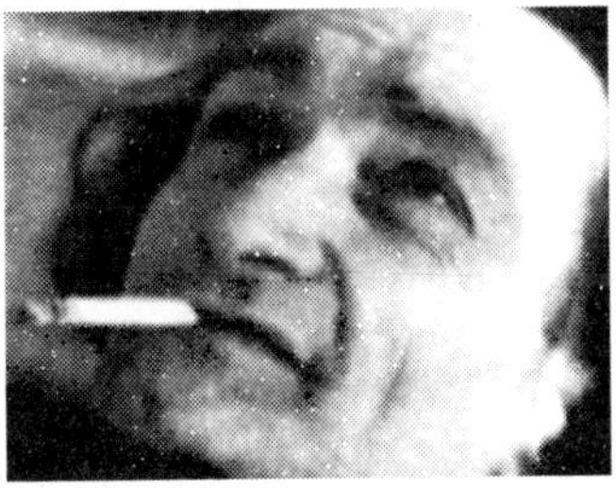

Antonin Artaud

Jerzy Grotowski

■ **theater of dionysus**

the outdoor theatre in Athens where Greek drama began as a part of religious rituals.

theater of the absurd

a post-World War II dramatic trend characterised by radical theatrical innovations. In works influenced by the Theatre of the absurd, non-traditional, sometimes-grotesque characterisations, plots and stage sets reveal a meaningless universe in which human values are irrelevant. Existentialist themes of estrangement, absurdity and futility link many of the works of this movement. The principal writers of the Theatre of the Absurd are Samuel Beckett, Eugene Ionesco, Jean Genet and Harold Pinter.

theater of the grotesque

an Italian theatrical movement characterised by plays written around the ironic and macabre aspects of daily life in the World War I era. Theatre of the Grotesque was named after the play 'The Mask and the Face' by Luigi Chiarelli, which was described as 'a grotesque in three acts'. The movement influenced the work of Italian dramatist Luigi Pirandello, author of Right You Are, If You Think You Are.

Also known as Teatro Grottesco.

thegn

a warrior who has sworn his loyalty to a lord in Anglo-Saxon society. In return for a gift of weaponry and provisions of food and drink at the Mead-hall, the thegn vows to fight for his lord and die in his service. He also takes up the task of avenging his lord's death if that lord should die.

theme

a central idea or statement that unifies and controls the entire work. The theme can take the form of a brief and meaningful insight or a comprehensive vision of life; it may be a single idea such as 'progress' (in many Victorian works), 'order and duty' (in many early Roman works), 'seize-the-day' (in many late Roman works), or 'jealousy' (in Shakespeare's Othello). The theme may also be a more complicated doctrine, such as Milton's theme in Paradise Lost, 'to justify the ways of God to men' or 'Socialism is the only sane reaction to the labour abuses in Chicago meat-packing plants' (Upton Sinclair's 'The Jungle'). A theme is the author's way of communicating and sharing ideas, perceptions and feelings with readers and it may be directly stated in the book, or it may only be implied.

thesis

a thesis is both an essay and the point argued in the essay. Thesis novels and thesis plays share the quality of containing a thesis, which is supported through the action of the story. A master's thesis and a doctoral dissertation are two theses required of graduate students.

thing

the thing was the closest approximation the Icelandic Vikings had to local government/court systems/police. The thing was a gathering of representatives from the local area to vote on policy, hear complaints, settle disputes and proclaim incorrigible individuals as outlaws.

■ third person

see **point of view.**

■ third wall

sometimes referred to as the 'fourth wall' depending upon how a stage builder numbers the sides of the stage, the third or fourth wall is an imaginary barrier that separates the events on stage from the audience. The idea is that the stage background is constructed with a cutaway view of the house, so that the people sitting on the audience can look through this invisible 'fourth wall' and look directly into the events inside. Such stages preclude theatre-in-the-round and require a modified arena stage set up with an expensive reproduction of an entire house or building, often complete with stairs, wallpaper, furniture and other bits to add verisimilitude. This type of stage became increasingly common within the last two centuries, but the money involved in constructing such stages often precludes their use in drama, leaving arena stages most popular for the architectural design of the stage.

■ Thomas Gray (1716-1771)

Thomas Gray was an English poet. In 1742 he wrote his first important poems such as *To Spring, On a Distant Prospect of Eton College* and a sonnet on the death of his close friend Richard West. He finished his great *Elegy Written in a Country Churchyard* in 1751. It is a meditative poem presenting thoughts conjured up by the sight of a rural graveyard. It is perhaps the most quoted poem in English. Walpole published Gray's Pindaric odes, *The Progress of Poesy* and *The Bard* in 1757. Gray's verse illustrates the evolution of English poetry in the 18th century. His poems range from the classicism of the 1742 poems to the romantic tendencies of *The Fatal Sisters* and *The Descent of Odin* (1768). Most of his verses were tinged with melancholy and even more of it reflects his extensive learning. He did not write large amount of poetry but his letters, which contain much humour, are among the finest in the English language.

■ Thomas Hardy (1840–1928)

Thomas Hardy was an English novelist and poet. He was born near Dorchester. His name is remembered amongst the great English writers of the 19th century. He served as assistant to Arthur Blomfield, a London architect from 1862 to 1867. Ill health forced him to return to Dorset, where he worked for Hicks and his successor until 1874. After the appearance of *Far From the Madding Crowd* (1874), popular as well as critical acclaim enabled him to devote himself exclusively to writing. In 1874, he married Emma Lavinia Gifford.

Over the next 22 years Hardy wrote many novels. His major works are

The Return of the Native (1878), *The Mayor of Casterbridge* (1886), *Tess of the D'Urbervilles* (1891) and *Jude the Obscure* (1896), the latter two considered masterpieces.

His poetry is spare, unadorned and unromantic and its pervasive theme is man's futile struggle against cosmic forces. In 1914 he married Florence Emily Dugdale, a children's book writer, some 40 years his junior. He spent the latter half of his life in Dorset and died there. His ashes are interred in Westminster Abbey, but his heart is buried separately, with a certain dark propriety, near the Egdon Heath.

■ threnody

see **dirge.**

■ tiring house

an enclosed area in an Elizabethan theatre where the actors awaited their cue to go on stage, changed their costumes and stored stage props.

■ tmesis

the division of a compound word into two parts, with one or more words between, as 'what place soever' for 'whatsoever'.

■ tone

the means of creating a relationship or conveying an attitude. By looking carefully at the choices an author makes (in characters, incidents, setting; in the work's stylistic choices and diction, etc.), careful readers often can isolate the tone of a work and sometimes infer from it the underlying attitudes that control and colour the story or poem as a whole. For instance, two different novelists might write stories about capitalism. Author #1 creates a tale in which an impoverished but hard-working young lad pulls himself out of the slums when he applies himself to his education and he becomes a wealthy, contented middle-class citizen who leaves his past behind him, never looking back at that awful human cesspool from which he rose. Author #2 creates a tale in which a dirty streetrat skulks his way out of the slums by abandoning his family and going off to college and he greedily hoards his money in a gated community and ignores the suffering of his former 'equals' whom he leaves behind in his selfish desire to get ahead. Note that both author #1 and author #2 are basically presenting the same plotline, but the first author's writing creates a tale of optimism and hope, but the second author shapes the same tale into a story of bitterness and cynicism. The difference is in their respective tones—the way they convey their attitudes about particular characters and subject matter.

■ tragedy

a serious play in which the chief figures, by some peculiarity of character, pass through a series of misfortunes leading to a final, devastating catastrophe. According to Aristotle, catharsis is the marking feature and ultimate end of any tragedy. He writes in his 'Poetics' (c. 350

BCE) 'Tragedy is an imitation of an action that is serious, complete and of a certain magnitude; . . . through pity (pathos) and fear effecting the proper purgation (Catharsis) of these emotions' (Book 6.2). Traditionally, a tragedy is divided into five acts. The first act introduces the characters in a state of happiness, or at the height of their power, influence, or fame. The second act typically introduces a problem or dilemma, which reaches a point of crisis in the third act, but which can still be successfully averted. In the fourth act, the main characters fail to avert or avoid the impending crisis or catastrophe and this disaster occurs. The fifth act traditionally reveals the grim consequences of that failure.

■ tragedy of blood

see **revenge tragedy.**

■ tragic flaw

in a tragedy, the quality within the hero or heroine which leads to his or her downfall.

Examples of the tragic flaw include Othello's jealousy and Hamlet's indecisiveness, although most great tragedies defy such simple interpretation.

■ tragic hero

see **hamartia.**

■ tragicomedy

an experimental Renaissance literary work—either a play or prose piece of fiction—containing elements common to both comedies and tragedies.

■ transcendentalism

an American philosophical and religious movement, based in New England from around 1835 until the Civil War. Transcendentalism was a form of American romanticism that had its roots abroad in the works of Thomas Carlyle, Samuel Coleridge and Johann Wolfgang von Goethe. The Transcendentalists stressed the importance of intuition and subjective experience in communication with God. They rejected religious dogma and texts in favour of mysticism and scientific naturalism. They pursued truths that lie beyond the 'colourless' realms perceived by reason and the senses and were active social reformers in public education, women's rights and the abolition of slavery.

Prominent members of the group include Ralph Waldo Emerson and Henry David Thoreau.

■ translatio

a Latin word, derived from the verb translatere, 'to carry beyond'. Translatio is the act of taking an older text in a different language and creating a new work that embodies the same ideas in a new language. Unlike modern translation, in which a translator tries to convey each sentence, word and phrase as literally and accurately as possible, the medieval idea of translatio was to take the gist of the original work's ideas and to convey them loosely in a new form. Examples include King

Alfred and Chaucer's 'translations' of Boethius' 'Consolation of Philosophy', Chaucer's loose 'translations' (i.e., new versions) of the Troy myth in Troilus and Criseyde adapted from earlier medieval Italian authors, or his abbreviated version of the French poem, Roman de la Rose. Medieval translators felt little compunction about keeping the same sequence of events, settings, or characters in their translations. The important element to be conveyed was the feeling and philosophy behind the original work.

■ travel literature

writings that describe either the author's journey to a distant and alien place, or which discuss the customs, habits and wildlife of a distant place. The oldest surviving travel literature is an account from 1300 BCE, an anonymous record of Egyptian naval voyages called 'The Journeying of the Master of the Captains of Egypt'. Herodotus' 'Histories' recount his travels in Egypt, Africa and elsewhere in the late 400s BCE. In China, we find accounts of travels to India by a certain Fa-Hian (c. 400 CE) and Shuman Hwui-Li's travels to the farthest Eastern reaches of the Chinese Empire. Roman travel literature includes writings by Gaius Solinus (c. 250 CE).

■ trench poetry

poetry and songs written by both poets and common soldiers that focussed on the disillusionment, suffering and ethical dismay these individuals felt at their involvement in World War I. The poetry is often bitter in tone. Often the poetic voice of the speaker mimics the voice, style and speech of an ordinary soldier. Sometimes the poet presents the poem's speaker in the persona of a soldier, even if the poet himself was not one. Much of this 'trench poetry' was published in trench newsletters. The well-known trench poets of the period include Sassoon. Owens' 'Dulce Et Decorum Est' is one famous example of trench poetry.

■ trial by combat

a means of resolving disputes between knights in which both agree to meet at an agreed-upon time and place and fight with agreed-upon weapons. The knight who was in the right and honest in his words would be the one to win the day, since in popular medieval theology, it was thought that God would favour the just. In actual point of fact, the late medieval church condemned trial by combat as barbaric, though records of it persist through the early 1300s. The habit of gentlemanly duels, which continued through the Renaissance, the Enlightenment and the Early Romantic period, along with the Western American practice of the gun-fight, are vague remnants of this earlier practice among knights. Shakespeare reveals examples of this ritual in the opening scenes of 'Richard II'.

■ tribrach

a metrical foot of three short syllables.

■ trickster

a character or figure common in Native American and African literature who uses his ingenuity to defeat enemies and escape difficult situations. Tricksters are most often animals, such as the spider, hare, or coyote, although they may take the form of humans as well. Examples of trickster tales include Thomas King's 'A Coyote Columbus Story', Ashley F. Bryan's 'The Dancing Granny' and Ishmael Reed's 'The Last Days of Louisiana Red'.

■ tricolon

the repetition of a parallel grammatical construction three times in a row for rhetorical effect.

■ trilogy

a group of three literary works that together compose a larger narrative. One of the earliest types of trilogy was the common practice of Athenian playwrights, who would submit tragedies as groups of three plays for performance in the Dionysia.

■ trimeter

a line consisting of three metrical feet. This short line is most common in English nursery rhymes, lullabies and children's songs.

■ triolet

a poem or stanza of eight lines in which the first line is repeated as the fourth and seventh lines and the second line as the eighth, with a rhyme scheme of ABaAabAB.

■ triple rhyme

a rhyme in which three final syllables of words have the same sound, as in 'glorious' and 'victorious'.

■ trisyllable

a word of three syllables.

■ trochee or trochaic

a metrical foot with a long or accented syllable followed by a short or unaccented syllable, as in 'only' or 'total', or the opening line of Poe's 'The Raven,'

■ troilus verse

see **rhyme royal.**

■ trope

the intentional use of a word or expression figuratively, i.e., used in a different sense from its original significance in order to give vividness or emphasis to an idea. Some important types of trope are: antonomasia, irony, metaphor, metonymy and synecdoche.

■ troubadour

a class of lyric poets and poet-musicians, often of knightly rank, who flourished from the 11th through the 13th centuries in Southern France and neighbouring areas of Italy and Spain and who wrote of courtly love.

■ trouvere

a school of poets of northern France who flourished from the

11th to 14th centuries and who composed mostly narrative works such as 'chansons de geste' and 'fabliaux'.

■ true rhyme

see **perfect rhyme.**

■ ubi sunt

poetic theme in which the poet asks 'where are' they, where have they gone. The theme began in Medieval Latin, with the formula ubi sunt used to introduce a roll-call of the dead or missing and to suggest how transitory life is.

■ understatement

see **irony.**

■ unities

strict rules of dramatic structure, formulated by Italian and French critics of the Renaissance and based loosely on the principles of drama discussed by Aristotle in his 'Poetics'. Foremost among these rules were the three unities of action, time and place that compelled a dramatist to: (1) construct a single plot with a beginning, middle and end that details the causal relationships of action and character; (2) restrict the action to the events of a single day; and (3) limit the scene to a single place or city. The unities were observed faithfully by continental European writers until the Romantic Age, but they were never regularly observed in English drama. Modern dramatists are typically more concerned with a unity of impression or emotional effect than with any of the classical unities.

The unities are observed in Pierre Corneille's tragedy 'Polyeuctes' and Jean-Baptiste Racine's 'Phedre'.

Also known as Three Unities.

■ unmetered poetry

poetry without a regular recurring numerical principle in its rhythmic construction, also known as 'free verse'.

■ unstressed syllable

a syllable that is not emphasised, like the 'a' in 'aghast' or the 'ish' in 'churlish'.

■ urban realism

a branch of realist writing that attempts to accurately reflect the often harsh facts of modern urban existence.

Some works by Stephen Crane, Theodore Dreiser, Charles Dickens, Fyodor Dostoyevsky, Emile Zola, Abraham Cahan and Henry Fuller feature urban realism. Modern examples include Claude Brown's 'Manchild in the Promised Land' and Ron Milner's 'What the Wine Sellers Buy'.

Charles Dickens

■ **utopia**

a fictional perfect place, such as 'paradise' or 'heaven'.

Early literary utopias were included in Plato's 'Republic' and Sir Thomas More's 'Utopia', while more modern utopias can be found in Samuel Butler's 'Erewhon', Theodor Herzka's 'A Visit to Freeland', H. G. Wells' 'A Modern Utopia' and Charlotte Perkins Gilman's 'Herland'.

■ **utopianism**

see **utopia.**

■ **V. S. Naipaul (1932–)**

Sir Vidiadhar Surajprasad Naipaul known as V.S. Naipaul is an English author, born in Chaguanas, Trinidad and graduated from University College, Oxford, 1953. Naipul has lived in England since 1950. A master of English prose style, he is known for his penetrating analyses of alienation and exile. Writing with increasing irony and pessimism, he has often bleakly detailed the dual problems of the Third World.Naipaul's

works of international analysis include *The Middle Passage* (1962), about the West Indies and South America and an Indian trilogy: *An Area of Darkness* (1964), *India: A Wounded Civilisation* (1977) and *India: A Million Mutinies Now* (1990). His novels include *The Mystic Masseur* (1957), *A House for Mr. Biswas* (1961), *In a Free State* (1971, Booker Prize), *Guerrillas* (1975), *A Bend in the River* (1979) and *Half a Life* (2001). He has also written *The Enigma of Arrival* (1987) and *A Way in the World* (1994), autobiographical works that combine novel, memoir and history. Naipaul was knighted in 1990 and awarded the Nobel Prize in Literature in 2001.

■ **verisimilitude**

literally, the appearance of truth. In literary criticism, the term refers to aspects of a work of literature that seem true to the reader.

Verisimilitude is achieved in the work of Honore de Balzac, Gustave Flaubert and Henry James, among other late nineteenth-century realist writers.

■ **vers libre**

see **free verse.**

■ **verse**

a line of writing arranged in a metrical pattern, i.e., a line of poetry. Also, a piece of poetry or a particular form of poetry such as free verse, blank verse, etc., or the art or work of a poet.

■ **verse paragraph**

a line grouping of varying length, as distinct from stanzas of equal length. Seldom used in rhymed verse, it is the usual division in blank verse.

■ **verset**

a short verse, especially one from a sacred book.

■ **versicle**

a little verse; also, a short passage said or sung by a leader in public worship and followed by a response from the people.

■ versification

the art of writing verses, especially with regard to meter and rhythm. The term versification can also refer to a particular metrical structure or style or to a version in verse of something originally written in prose.

■ versifier

a writer of verse, often applied to a writer of light or inferior verse.

■ Victor Marie Vicomte Hugo (1802–85)

Victor Marie was French poet, dramatist and novelist, born in Besançon. His father was a general under Napoleon. As a child he was taken to Italy and Spain and at a very early age had published his first book of poems, resolving to be Chateaubriand or nothing. The preface to his drama *Cromwell* (1827) placed him at the head of the romanticists. His principal poetic works are *Les Orientales* (1829), *Les Feuilles d'automne* (1831), *Les Chants du crépuscule* (1835), *Les Voix intérieures* (1837) and *La Légende des siècles* (1859). The production of his poetic drama *Hernani*, caused a riot between the classicists and the romanticists. His other important novels include *Les Travailleurs de la mer* (1866) and *Quatre-vingt-treize* (1874). He began his political career as a supporter of the duke of Reichstadt, Napoleon's son. Later Hugo espoused the cause of Louis Philippe's son and then for a short time of Louis Bonaparte. Because he afterward opposed Napoleon III, Hugo was banished. In 1870 he returned to Paris in triumph. He was elected for the national assembly and the senate. His last years were marked by public veneration and acclaim and he was buried in the Panthéon.

■ Victorian

refers broadly to the reign of Queen Victoria of England (1837-1901) and to anything with qualities typical of that era. For example, the qualities of smug narrow-mindedness, bourgeois materialism, faith in social progress and priggish morality are often considered Victorian. This stereotype is contradicted by such dramatic intellectual developments as the theories of Charles Darwin, Karl Marx and Sigmund Freud (which stirred strong debates in England) and the critical attitudes of serious Victorian writers like Charles Dickens and George Eliot. In literature, the Victorian Period was the great age of the English novel and the latter part of the era saw the rise of movements such as decadence and symbolism.

Works of Victorian literature include the Poetry of Robert Browning and Alfred, Lord Tennyson, the criticism of Matthew Arnold and John Ruskin and the novels of Emily Bronte, William Makepeace Thackeray and Thomas Hardy.

Also known as Victorian Age and Victorian Period.

■ Victorian age

see **victorian**

■ Victorian period

see **victorian**

■ Vikram Seth

Vikram Seth's writings are greatly influenced by his experiences of India, China and America. His best-known work is the novel *A Suitable Boy*, published in 1993.

He was born in Calcutta (now Kolkata) to Hindu parents. He was educated at English schools in India prior to attending Corpus Christi College at the University of Oxford, in England. He received a B.A. degree from Oxford, M.A. degrees from Stanford University, in California and Oxford and a graduate study diploma from Nanjing University in Eastern China.

Seth's early works include the poetry collection *The Humble Administrator's Garden* (1983) and a travel journal of a hitchhiking trip, *From Heaven Lake: Travels Through Sinkiang and Tibet* (1983). He wrote the novel *The Golden Gate* (1986) in verse form, as a series of sonnets. It focuses on a group of young California professionals in the 1980s. Other works include the poetry volume *All You Who Sleep Tonight* (1990) and a children's book of retellings of traditional poetry and fables, *Beastly Tales from Here and There* (1992).

In 1993 *A Suitable Boy* was published to great acclaim. The book, which won one of Britain's annual literary prizes, the W. H. Smith Award, is the story of an Indian mother's search for a suitable match for her daughter. The tale is set against the panoramic backdrop of life in India just after the country gained independence from Britain in 1947.

Seth took on a new literary form with the *Libretto Arion and the Dolphin* (1994), a retelling of the story of Greek poet Arion being saved from drowning by a dolphin. The libretto was published to coincide with the first performance of an opera of the same name, with music by English composer Alec Roth, at the English National Opera in London, in 1994. Seth returned to the novel form with *An Equal Music* (1999), which depicts a love affair between two musicians.

■ villanelle

a poem in a fixed form, consisting of five three-line stanzas followed by a quatrain and having only two rhymes. In the stanzas following the first, the first and third lines of the first stanza are repeated alternately as refrains. They are the final two lines of the concluding quatrain.

■ virelay

an ancient French verse form consisting of stanzas of indeterminate length and number, with alternating long and short lines and an interlaced rhyme scheme, as abab bcbc cdcd dada.

■ Virginia Woolf (Stephen) (1882–1941)

Virginia Woolf was the daughter of Sir Leslie Stephen. She was an English novelist and essayist. She is considered as a successful innovator in the form of the novel fiction. She was educated at home from the resources of her father's huge library. In 1912, she married Leonard Woolf, a critic and writer on economics, with whom she set up the Hogarth Press in 1917. As a novelist Woolf's emphasis was not on plot or characterisation but on a character's consciousness, his thoughts and feelings. She did not limit herself to one consciousness, however, but slipped from mind to mind, particularly in *The Waves*, probably her most experimental novel. Woolf's early works, *The Voyage Out* (1915) and *Night and Day* (1919), were traditional in method, but she became increasingly innovative in *Jacob's Room* (1922), *Mrs. Dalloway* (1925), *To the Lighthouse* (1927) and *The Waves* (1931).

Virginia Woolf suffered mental breakdowns in 1895 and 1915. She drowned herself in 1941 because she feared another breakdown from which she might not recover.

■ visual poetry

poetry arranged in such a manner that its visual appearance has an elevated significance of its own, thus achieving in an equivalence (or even more) between the sight and sound of the poem.

■ voice

the agent or agency who is speaking throughout a poem.

■ volta

the place at which a distinct turn of thought occurs. The term is most commonly used for the characteristic transition point in a sonnet, as between the octave and sestet of a Petrarchan sonnet.

■ vowel rhyme

see **assonance.**

■ W. B. Yeats (1865-1939)

W. B. Yeats, Irish poet and playwright, one of the major figures of 20th-century literature and the greatest lyric poet Ireland has produced. Yeats was the acknowledged leader of the Irish literary renaissance. Yeats' verse can be divided into two periods. The first one was from 1886 to about 1900. At this time the prevailing theme in his poetry was Irish mythology. Some of the best-known poems of the period are *Falling of Leaves*, *When You Are Old* and *The Lake Isle of Innisfree*. Yeats's poetry deepened, as he grew older. His poetry became stronger, more physical and realistic. Memorable poems from this period include *The Second Coming*, *The Tower* and *Sailing to Byzantium*. Yeats' prose tales were collected in *The Celtic Twilight* (1893) and in the symbolic *Secret Rose* (1897). Yeats initiated his second period in such volumes as *In the Seven Woods* (1903) and *The Green Helmet and Other Poems* (1910). Some of his best works were his last, *The Tower* (1928) and *Last Poems* (1940). Yeats won the Nobel Prize in Literature in 1923.

■ W. H. Auden (1907-1973)

W. H. Auden studied at Oxford and was an Anglo-American poet. Auden ranks among the major literary figures of the 20th century because of his versatile, vigorous and technically superior skills. His poetry ranges from politics to modern psychology to Christianity. During the 1930 Auden was the leader of the left-wing literary group and during this time only his first volume of poetry appeared. Auden wrote four verse plays with Isherwood namely *The Dog beneath the Skin* (1935), *The Ascent of F6* (1936) and *On the Frontier* (1938) and *Journey to a War* (1939). During the Spanish Civil War he was the stretcher- bearer for the republicans. His later volumes include *Spain* (1937), *New Year Letter* (1941), *For the Time Being, A Christmas Oratorio* (1945), *The Age of Anxiety* (1947, Pulitzer Prize), *Nones* (1951), *The Shield of Achilles* (1955), *Homage to Clio* (1960), *About the House* (1965), *Epistle of a Godson and Other Poems* (1972) and *Thank You, Fog* (1974). His other works include *Letters from Iceland* (with Louis MacNeice, 1937), *The Libretto*, with his companion Chester Kallman, for Stravinsky's opera *The Rake's Progress* (1953), *A Certain World: A Commonplace Book* (1970) and *The Dyer's Hand and Other Essays* (1968). He was awarded the National Medal for Literature in 1967.

■ Walter Benjamin (1892–1940)

Benjamin was a German essayist and critic. He is known for his synthesis of eccentric Marxist theory and Jewish messianism. His essays on Charles Baudelaire and Franz Kafka as well as his theory on symbolism, allegory and the function of art in a mechanical age have deeply affected contemporary criticism. In the collection of his works, Walter Benjamin demonstrates complete adherence to the notion of history moving through the necessary epochs set forth by Marx, to human material desire being the prime mover of mankind, to the notions of alienation and to the proletariat being the class with the ability to move mankind (through revolution) from the current epoch of capitalism, to the next epoch, communism. Benjamin's method is a combination of an artful use of literary tools, empirical observation and inspirational experience.

Benjamin was influenced by his close friendship with the historian of Jewish mysticism

Gershom Gerhard Scholem. In 1933, he moved to France because of the rise of the Nazis. When the Nazis invaded France, he fled to Spain. He was denied entry into the country so he committed suicide.

■ **wedge verse**

see **rhopalic.**

■ **well-versed**

a state of familiarity with poetics.

■ **weltanschauung**

a German term referring to a person's World View or philosophy.

W. H. Auden

Examples of weltanschauung include Thomas Hardy's view of the human being as the victim of fate, destiny, or impersonal forces and circumstances and the disillusioned and laconic cynicism expressed by such poets of the 1930s as W. H. Auden, Sir Stephen Spender and Sir William Empson.

William Empson

■ **weltschmerz**

a German term meaning 'world pain'. It describes a sense of anguish about the nature of existence, usually associated with a melancholy. pessimistic attitude.

Weltschmerz was expressed in England by George Gordon, Lord Byron in his Manfred and Childe Harold's Pilgrimage, in France by Viscount de Chateaubriand, Alfred de Vigny and Alfred de Musset, in Russia by Aleksandr Pushkin and Mikhail Lermontov, in Poland by Juliusz Slowacki and in America by Nathaniel Hawthorne.

■ **whimsy or whimsey**

a fanciful or fantastic creation in writing or art.

■ **William Blake (1757-1827)**

William Blake, English poet and artist. He was a poet who was sensitive and responsive to the realities of the human conditions of his time. Blake spent all his life in London except for three years at Felpham where he prepared illustrations for an edition of Cowper. *Poetical Sketches* was the only book published during his lifetime. In *Songs of Innocence* (1789) and *Songs of Experience* (1794) the world is seen from a child's point of view, directly and simply but without sentimentality. The first group contains poems like *The Lamb, Infant, Joy* and *Laughing Songs*. Both the beauty and the pain of life are captured. The latter group, which includes *The Tiger, Infant, Sorrow, The Sick Rose* and *London* reveal a consciousness of cruelty and injustice in the world, for which people, not fate, are responsible. Blake wrote Prophetic Books such as *The Book of Thel* (1789), *The Marriage of Heaven and Hell* (1790), *The French Revolution* (1791), *America* (1793), *Europe* (1794), *The Book of Urizon* (1794), *The Book of Los* (1795), *Milton* (1804–8) and *Jerusalem* (1804–20). Blake exalted love and pure liberty and abhorred the reductive, rationalist philosophy.

■ William Cowper (1731-1800)

William Cowper was an English poet. He was unfit for the professional life both physically and emotionally. He met John Newton, the ardent evangelical preacher in Olney. He contributed to *Newton's Olney Hymns* (1779) several poems, including the two commencing *Oh for a closer walk with God* and *God moves in a mysterious way*. After recovering from another period of insanity Cowper turned to writing about simple homely subjects, producing his famous long poem, *The Task* (1785). Its descriptions of the sights and sounds of country life foreshadowed 19th-century romanticism. *The Diverting History of John Gilpin* shows Cowper's sweet-tempered, playful moods that found a way into many of his other poems. After the death of Mrs. Unwin in 1796, he wrote little except the anguished poem, *The Castaway*.

■ William Empson (1906-1984)

William Empson, English critic and poet, wrote modern literary criticism and a notable book on this theme of criticism is *His Seven Types of Ambiguity*, a study of the meanings of poetry. It was published in 1930.Other books of Empson are *Some Versions of Pastoral* (1935) and *The Structure of Complex Words* (1951). Empson attacked Puritanism in his book *Milton's God,* which was published in 1961. He also wrote poems, which were noteworthy for their wit and metaphysical conceits like *Poems* (1935) and *The Gathering Storm* (1940). His collected edition of poems was published in 1955. He was knighted in 1979

■ William Joyce (1906–46)

William Joyce was born in Brooklyn, N.Y. He was a British Nazi propagandist and titled as Lord Haw-Haw. Taken to England as a child, Joyce became involved there in the fascist movement. He went to Germany just before the outbreak of World War II and throughout the war broadcast German propaganda in English from Berlin. Friends in Germany put Joyce in contact with Dr. Erich Hetzler - Private Secretary to Germany's Foreign Minister von Ribbentrop. Two weeks after the outbreak of war he was appointed Editor and speaker for the German transmitters for Europe at Berlin's Charlottenburg. Joyce was still only 33 years old. His wartime broadcasts to England became infamous - he was nicknamed *Lord Haw-Haw* by a *Daily Express* journalist because of his aristocratic nasal drawl. Unknown to the public at this time, his image was very different from the scar-faced fascist thug he was usually portrayed as.

British soldiers in Germany captured him in 1945. Despite his American birth, he was adjudged subject to British jurisdiction because he held a British passport. He was convicted of treason and hanged.

■ William Morris (1834-1896)

William Morris, English poet, artist, craftsman, designer, social reformer and printer. He was called the greatest English designer of the 19th century and was considered one of the great Victorians. In 1858 he published his first volume of poems, *The Defense of Guenevere and Other Poems* and after that *The Life and Death of Jason* (1867) and *The Earthly Paradise* (1868–70). After joining politics Morris wrote his two notable prose works *The Dream of John Ball* (1888) and *News from Nowhere* (1891). His last artistic venture and one of his most important, was the *Kelmscott Press* in Hammersmith. This press was established in 1890 where he designed the type, page borders and bindings of fine books. Morris made a profound effect on the printing industry with his brilliant graphic and elegant designs. He was a famous poet in his time but is not read widely by people today.

■ William Rose Benét (1886-1950)

William Rose Benet, American poet and editor. He was the brother of Stephen Vincent Benét. He worked at the *Century Magazine* and the *Literary Review of the* New *York Evening Post* as an editor or assistant editor. The *Saturday Review of Literature* was founded in 1924 with his help and he also worked as an editor here. His books include collections of poetry such as *Merchants from Cathay* (1913), *The Great White Wall* (1916) and *Man Possessed* (1927). He wrote novels like *The First Person Singular* (1922), *Wild Goslings* (1927) and *The Reader's Encyclopaedia* (1948). He also co-edited *The Oxford Anthology of American Literature* (1938). His second wife was the poet, Elinor Wylie, whose poems he edited in 1932. *The Dust Which Is God* (1941), won the 1942

Pulitzer Prize in poetry, it was his autobiographical narrative.

■ William Shakespeare (1564–1616)

William Shakespeare is one of the most celebrated English dramatist and poet, born in Stratford-on-Avon. He is considered the greatest playwright who ever lived.

He probably attended the grammar school in Stratford, where he would have been educated in the classics, particularly Latin grammar and literature. In 1582 Shakespeare married Anne Hathaway, eight years his senior and pregnant at the time of the marriage. In 1594 Shakespeare became an actor and playwright for the company Lord Chamberlain's Men. As an actor he played old men's roles, such as the ghost in Hamlet and Old Adam in As You Like It. His first plays are believed to be the three parts of Henry VI. After these come *The Comedy of Errors, Titus Andronicus, The Taming of the Shrew, The Two Gentlemen of Verona, Love's Labour's Lost* and *Romeo and Juliet.*

Shakespeare also wrote *A Midsummer Night's Dream, King John, The Merchant of Venice, Julius Caesar, As You Like It* and *Twelfth Night.* His plays—*Pericles, Cymbeline, The Winter's Tale* and *The Tempest*—are tragicomedies. Shakespeare's first published poems were *Venus and Adonis* (1593) and *The Rape of Lucrece* (1594). Shakespeare's sonnets are by far his most important non-dramatic poetry.

■ William Wordsworth (1770-1850)

William Wordsworth is regarded as one of the greatest English poets. He was a leader of the Romantic Movement in England. *An Evening Walk* and *Descriptive Sketches* were published in 1793. Wordsworth's earlier work shows the poetic beauty of commonplace things and people as in *Margaret, Peter Bell, Michael* and *The Idiot Boy.*

Along with Coleridge he wrote *Lyrical Ballads* in 1798, this book included Wordsworth's poem *Tintern Abbey.* Second edition of *Lyrical Ballads* was published in 1800. *The Prelude,* his long autobiographical poem, was completed in 1805, though it was not published until after his death. His next collection, *Poems in Two Volumes* (1807), included the well-known *Ode to Duty* and *Ode: Intimations of Immortality* and a number of famous sonnets. Some of his other notable poems are *The Excursion* (1814), *Laodamia* (1815), *White Doe of Rylstone* (1815), *Memorials of a Tour of the Continent, 1820* (1822) and *Yarrow Revisited* (1835). He was named poet laureate. He was regarded as an original thinker who created a new poetic tradition.

■ wordsmith

a person who works with words; a skilful writer.

wrenched accent

a forced change in the normal accent of a word syllable(s) to make the word conform to the prevailing metrical pattern. While it may result from faulty versification, it was conventional in the folk ballad and is sometimes used deliberately for comic effects.

zarzuela

a type of Spanish operetta. Writers of zarzuelas include Lope de Vega and Pedro Calderon.

zeitgeist

a German term meaning 'spirit of the time'. It refers to the moral and intellectual trends of a given era.

zeugma

a figure of speech in which a single word, usually a verb or adjective, is used in the same grammatical and semantic relationship with two or more other words.

33. Geology	95/-
34. Genetic Engineering	95/-
35. Health & Nutrition	95/-
36. History	95/-
37. Import and Export	95/-
38. Information System Management	95/-
39. Internet	95/-
40. IT	95/-
41. Inorganic Chemistry	95/-
42. Law	95/-
43. Library & Information Science	95/-
44. Literature	95/-
45. Management	95/-
46. Mathematics	95/-
47. Marketing & Sales	95/-
48. Mass Communication	95/-
49. Mechanical Engg.	95/-
50. Medical	95/-
51. Music	95/-
52. Organic Chemistry	95/-
53. Philosophy	95/-
54. Physical Education	95/-
55. Physics	95/-
56. Psychology	95/-
57. Science	95/-
58. Sex	95/-
59. Sociology	95/-
60. Sports	95/-
61. Textile	95/-
62. Zoology	95/-

Lotus PRESS

Unit No. 220, Second Floor, 4735/22,
Prakash Deep Building, Ansari Road, Darya Ganj,
New Delhi - 110002, Ph.: 32903912, 23280047, 09811594448
E-mail: lotus_press@sify.com, www.lotuspress.co.in

Notes

Notes